RALPH READER REMEMBERS

RALPH READER REMEMBERS

RALPH READER C.B.E.

BAILEY BROTHERS & SWINFEN LTD
FOLKESTONE

Published in Great Britain by
Bailey Brothers and Swinfen Ltd
1974

ISBN 561 00242 8

Printed in Great Britain by
Kingprint Limited, Richmond, Surrey

To:

Bob, Joan, William and Stephen without whom ....

Toby

Contents

The story of one life, told by the man who says:—
"It's all been worth it!"

1

One Life

The only way to start a story is to begin at the beginning, so let me kick off with a profound statement. I was born!

The place was a small, charming little town in Somerset, England, and its name is Crewkerne. The date was May the 25th, 1903. So right away I have proved that I am English, and it needs proving because of an accent I have accumulated through the years, having lived in Somerset, Sussex, Wales, Ireland, America, Canada and now London. Put that lot together and there can be no wonder that I am constantly asked, "Where the hell do you come from?" The answer is, "All over."

A cat has nine lives, a human being only one and the following pages are concerned with just that: one life – mine.

One life, nature's great leveller. It's the same for the captains and the kings, for the rich and the poor, for the weak and for the strong. Perhaps a lot depends on the bed you were born in, but much more depends on *you*.. Anyway, that's how I figure it and I've had a lot of years to do the figuring. I can look back without envy, with only gratitude. Times have sometimes been tough, but perhaps this did me no harm because it made me realise how good the brighter times could be. I have no desire to live my life over again – you can't be lucky twice – and if anyone asks me if I would like to be seventeen again I quickly tell them, "No, because nobody could guarantee that I'd be eighteen."

I was born into the poorest of families with a mother and a father who were Salvationists. All the rest of my relations were either Baptists, Wesleyans, Quakers, Gospel Hallers, one or two not quite certain, and naturally the more sedate ones Church of England. All of my relations were strict tee-totallers except at times of illness and it was always amazing how often they felt out of sorts. I remember one incident many years later when I went to Crewkerne to crown the Carnival Queen. We were given an excellent supper to end the celebrations, and about half past eleven, my Aunt Nell (of whom you will hear more later) walked into the Red Lion Hotel with a stern face and asked me, "Have you been imbibing?" I told her I had, and went on, "Now come and have a drink, it will do you good." She turned to me in horror and said, "How dare you! Never shall I soil my lips with the Demon drink. Not a single drop shall I ever . . ." She suddenly clutched my arm and exclaimed, "Oh, my heart, quick – a double brandy." She had four!

I was an orphan at nine and left school when I was eleven. I had a year in a school in Cardiff and there for the first time took part in a play which was, perhaps understandably, performed on St. David's Day. I was ten at the time and was cast as Bishop Morgan. I still don't know who Bishop Morgan was, and, according to Mr. Williams, our teacher, I didn't behave as becomes such a dignitary. "You were giggling all the time, Reader" he told me, "And bishops do NOT pick their noses in public." So much for my initial stage appearance.

At the beginning of World War One I went to live in a

tiny village near Newhaven and it was here, in Denton, that I joined the Scouts. Although at the time unknown and unsuspected by me, this began a way of life I was to follow for the rest of my days. There was only one small church in the village and so I became a member of the Church of England. I joined the choir and on certain Sunday mornings played the organ. I could only play with two fingers (never have had a lesson in my whole life) and though I didn't play very well I certainly played very loud. One major problem was the fact that I could play only in one key, and this caused difficulties. It meant that the tenors in the choir were often singing bass and the bass singers couldn't sing at all, so the best they could do was to glare down at me with a sadistic fiery fury which didn't daunt me one bit. I even played Jackson's "Te Deum" right through in the same key which any musician would regard as a miracle. By anyone at all musical it was referred to as purgatory. Fortunately a real organist was discovered and with her coming back came many of the congregation.

At fourteen I became a telegraph messenger and at fifteen I changed my job and became an office boy at a cement works, which was being used as a bomb disposal factory, and it was at this time I started putting on Scout Concerts for various war charities – which ones I never bothered to find out, as all I cared about was putting on concerts. War ended, the factory began to turn out cement again, and then came the depression. The manager was transferred to a branch in Northern Ireland and asked me if I would like to go with him as a junior clerk. He was perfectly aware that I was useless as any sort of clerk, but he thought I might be useful putting on concerts to cheer up the Ulstermen. I jumped at the opportunity and away I went. Seven months I stayed there, and to this day I can honestly say they were the happiest months of my life. The reason will be told later. Then a letter came to me from an aunt in America suggesting that I might like to try my luck in the States. She knew I was madly interested in the stage and she knew someone who knew someone who once got an autograph from an actor (or words to that effect), and she thought it might be the means of my getting into the theatre. (It was, but only by buying tickets to go in the front way to see the show). I left Ireland. I went to America.

Not even the bravest fortune-teller would have dared to prophecy what the years ahead were to bring me. I was just eighteen at the time and my first eighteen months in America were pure hell, BUT after that!! Before I was twenty-four I had become a name on Broadway, worked with practically every musical comedy and revue star on that Great White Way, played with Al Jolson and then became one of the top dance directors, with the New York critics hitting the headlines by christening me "The Kid Dance Director." *Variety* said, "Reader is only twenty-two; he has conceived the snappiest and most involved ensembles that have found their way to the stage." Walter Winchell wrote, "The new show that opened last night at the Winter Garden has a galaxy of stars but the brightest of all is the unseen dance director, Ralph Reader." Who could have foretold that I would be associated with twenty-two American musicals, play in various night-clubs (one with a juicy murder in the middle of a performance) and then return to England to produce thirty four shows in the West End and to work with Noël Coward, Gertrude Lawrence, Ivor Novello and every British music hall and musical comedy star of the day; to appear in four Royal Command Performances and then to suddenly sweep into the Royal Albert Hall where I was to produce over one hundred and forty presentations – some with a cast of over two thousand performers headed by such celebrities as Laurence Olivier, Flora Robson, Marlene Dietrich, Margot Fonteyn and that great conductor, Sir Malcolm Sargent. With Sir Malcolm I was to produce at the Royal Opera House, Covent Garden, *Pilgrim's Progress.* In between all these things I wrote and produced a three-night revue which we called *The Gang*

Show. It opened in October 1932 at the Scala Theatre just off Tottenham Court Road – over forty years ago and still to-day that show is being played in villages, towns and cities in all parts of the world. Even the 1939 war didn't stop its progress, for units of ten men were formed by the Royal Air Force to bring fun and cheer to serving men and women on every battle front where the war was being fought. Many of the young men who formed those units and whom I found in cook-houses, guard rooms and tiny R.A.F. stations all over the country are now world famous names. Peter Sellers, Dick Emery, Norrie Paramor, Harry Worth, Reg Dixon, Cardew Robinson and the late Tony Hancock are but a few.

But the story behind the *real* reason for forming these R.A.F. Gang Shows has never been told. It can be now!! Unknown to all but a few I was working under the immediate command of Air Commodore Archie Boyle who was then the Director of the R.A.F. Intelligence. These plans were laid just before the war and one of my early assignments was a meeting with a man named Ribbentrop. That was only the beginning.

I was demobbed as a Squadron Leader with an M.B.E., later to become a C.B.E., and here I am now nicely over the seventy mark with still plenty to do and in my spare moments I find time to re-cap the years gone by. Few men have more friends than I have been lucky enough to collect and no Christmas comes with fewer than two thousand cards arriving from all parts of the world.

I've had a varied career – and that's a slight understatement. Once I was so hungry when touring Canada with a very cheap "Stock Company" who could seldom pay our salaries that I crept out of my digs one night and went to a nearby farm, pulled swedes out of the ground and sat down and ate as many as I could. I have stayed for seven weeks in a super suite at the Savoy Hotel in London (paid for by the Daily Express); I once skipped out of a cheap night club in Brooklyn without a penny in my pocket to make my way back to New York, which I did by 'riding the rails', luckily undiscovered by the cops who were looking for just the likes of me. I have had the honour of lunching with Her Majesty the Queen at a private luncheon at Buckingham Palace and I have mixed with various characters from all walks of life. Capone, Legs Diamond and Baby-Face Nelson, and on the other side of the ledger, Earl Mountbatten. I remember the first time I saw him. It was in India and we were ordered to be at an early morning parade where he was to speak. About two hundred officers were gathered in a smallish room and we stood to attention as he entered and walked to a small platform raised about a foot from the floor. He mounted it and looked at us. Standing straight as a ram-rod, looking like the conning tower of a submarine and ready to release enough explosives to sink everything in sight, he spoke to us. Personality? No – magic! He was the Supremo and no more fitting title could there be for him. Years later (after the war) he was talking to me at the Albert Hall where we were staging a big Army Pageant. He turned to the Duke of Kent and said, "Eddy, I think we should call Reader the Impressario of the Services." I enjoyed that.

My first meeting with Air Chief Marshal Tedder is quite a story too, and I often remember the evening Lady Tedder took me to see Winston Churchill in a house not far from Tunis where he was recovering from pneumonia. It was immediately after his meeting with Stalin and Roosevelt. He was seated in a wheel chair and when I looked at his face, pale maybe but with the grim determination as fierce as ever, I knew we couldn't lose.

I shall tell later of my meeting with General Sikorski when he came to the R.A.F. Station, Eastchurch, where I had been sent to 'keep the Poles busy' as they arrived in England after escaping from their homeland to form here the new Polish Air Force, and why he said to me, "You are so popular with my men, Reader, I'm beginning to think you are after my job."

All in one life, and if it ends to-morrow I shall have no regrets, for nothing that has been can be taken away from me when the time comes for me to 'go'. I shall lose only the things that have never been, but what *has* been – the love, the friendships and all the good things I have been blessed with – are *mine* and I shall take them with me when I go.

Now let's get back to the start and tell the whole story.

2

My Family

There isn't a great deal I can tell you about my mother and father because they had both died before I reached the age of nine. That they were devout Christians I know and the early training I had from them has stood me in good stead throughout all the years of my life. Although I was only three years old, I still remember saying my prayers each night by my mother's bed where she lay dying of consumption. She was a very beautiful woman and the photographs I have of her make me realise what a lovely lady she was. My father was for a time bandmaster of the Crewkerne Corps of the Salvation Army. He wrote plays for them too but alas some of these didn't meet with the approval of certain Salvation Army officers and were considered 'too worldly'. It's quite likely they were! Dad was also a very fine instrumentalist – in fact he excelled in practically everything but making money. We kept a small shop in Goulds Barton, selling every kind of odds and ends from pins and needles to necklaces, cheap rings and even furniture which a few people bought and paid for at the rate of a shilling a week. The result was that the Christmas Dad died our gas was cut off immediately because the bills hadn't been paid for over a year.

Fatherless and motherless I might be, but comfort and protection were still mine. They came to me at the hands of someone whose memory I shall cherish until my own last day. I cannot remember a world without Annie Purchase: and what a bleak place it would have been without her. Annie lived with us and worked herself to a standstill for us. She came first of all, I suppose, as a servant – but after mother died she kept house for Dad and served in the shop. I never knew what Annie's wages were, but I do know they were rarely paid. Fiercely loyal, she stayed with us to the end and after the funeral she quietly assumed the role of my guardian and mother. Dear, compassionate Annie! I am sure it never occurred to her to do anything else. She would have been infinitely surprised to know what a profound impression her goodness made upon me.

From the moment I became an orphan it was a toss up as to whom I should live with so let me tell you about the relations closest to me at the time who could or might have 'taken me in'.

Dad had four sisters, each as different from the others as chalk from cheese – Jane, Liz, Rose and Nell. Aunt Jane I knew least of all because she lived nine miles away in Yeovil and it was only on occasions that we could afford the fare to visit her. So let's get on to the most interesting, and that means Aunt Rose! She had money – how much was always a talking point among the other sisters and the amount varied according to their imagination and, believe me, my family was never short of imagination. They excelled in it. But she was far from being broke, because she owned three houses in Nightingale Road, Clapton, and she and her husband, Will Hooper, lived in one of them. Uncle Will was a tram driver, and when he wasn't driving trams Aunt Rose was driving him. At odd times when I visited them for a week-end I soon discovered she knew all about economics. If, even in mid-winter, we went out for an hour, out came a small watering-can which sprinkled water on the coal fire putting it completely out. "Can't waste coal, dear" she used to say, and she certainly didn't. When you returned home the rule was to go straight to bed, and it was like sleeping in a deep freeze. I swear that one sack of coal would last her three or four winters.

Aunt Rose had one sadistic vice. She liked to recite. She knew more recitations than any woman had a right to know and she never lost an opportunity of getting up and going through them one by one whenever the mood took her, and the mood was always taking her. They were incredible poems about the wages of sin, deaths at sea, fires which scorched people (especially children) to cinders, and heroes and heroines who lost their lives in acts of bravery. If they didn't lose their lives the poems were no good. She also specialised in fallen women. One of her favourite pieces was called "Little Jim" and I well remember the opening lines:–

"The cottage was a thatched one,
The outside old and mean,
Yet everything within that cot
Was wondrous neat and clean. (End of verse one)
A crying mother knelt beside
The death-bed of her child – "

You can guess the rest and it always proved a winner – to Aunt Rose. Poor Jim died of course, otherwise the poem wouldn't have been included in her repertoire.

On Sunday nights she was in her glory for it was then that she visited Old People's Homes and held forth. I asked her once why she always spent her Sunday evenings this way and she replied, "Because, dear, they dear souls are so old." It never occurred to her that by the time she had finished her recital they all looked ten years older. Uncle Will always went with her to these 'concerts' and he knew all her recitations as well as she did. One night this knowledge was his undoing!

Aunt Rose lingered a little longer than usual after one verse before going on to the next and poor Uncle Will mistakenly thought she had forgotten the next line (as if she ever would), so he spoke it out loud to her as a 'prompt'. All present turned to see where the voice came from and then quickly turned back to look at Aunt Rose. She was smiling a smile at Uncle Will which shrivelled his liver and he knew at once he had made a mistake and would pay for it later. He wasn't disappointed – when they reached home she put him flat on his back.

However, Aunt Rose was genuinely fond of me and she constantly let it be known to all and sundry that when the time came for her to 'answer the call' everything she owned would come to me. The poor soul died three weeks before her husband so whatever was intended for me went to the other side of the family. I didn't even get the watering can.

The remaining two sisters, Liz and Nell, both lived in Crewkerne, in the same street but on different sides and in different environments. Let's take Liz first. She was married to Will Lye who had served in the Royal Navy. As far as I recall he reached the rank of petty officer but to all Crewkerne he was known as "Admiral Lye". This pleased him and I think he began to believe it, but I readily admit he looked every inch an Admiral when he walked down Market Street to the Conservative Club, always smartly dressed with his dignified bearing and his handsome bearded face. Aunt Liz, especially walking up South Street on Sunday mornings on her way to the Parish Church, also made a fine impression, particularly on me. She always seemed to be dressed in silk or satin, a beautiful black feather boa round her neck and a hat with a bird of multi-coloured plumage perched on top, determined to compete even with the hatpins. The 'lesser lights' on their way to the Wesleyan Chapel could do nothing but turn green with envy. The bird used to look so satisfied and so did Aunt Liz. The Lyes were a very large family but were far from being the millionaires I imagined them to be.

I didn't visit them a great deal, but every now and then I would call in to see them in their very charming house and a welcome was always waiting though I rarely got further than the kitchen. There were two other downstair rooms in this house, one leading from the kitchen and the other what is usually known as the front room. To get into either of these two rooms was an obsession with me because in each of them there was an upright piano. Oh how I longed to get to one or other of these pianos and play (with two fingers of course) – to just sit and *play*. It happened more than once, and there was one occasion which I shall never forget. I called one evening and they were having a small family conference, so to get me out of the way they took me into the front room and closed the door. It was a Thursday evening – you see I still remember which night of the week it was – and there I found myself alone with the piano in front of me. For a moment I held my breath. I could hardly believe my luck. I sat on the stool and played quietly at first (in case somebody came in and said "Not too loud, son"). I gathered confidence and played (if you will forgive the word) every hymn I could think of and then madly began trying out what I knew of the latest popular songs. Imagination began to get hold of me and I started to improvise, then I swayed back and forth on the stool rendering a concerto whilst thousands sat breathless listening to *me*. They were all dressed in evening clothes and the ladies were wearing diamonds and tiaras; their hands were clasped together and their fingers were loaded with rings which they wore instead of gloves. Mother Nature brought me back to earth. I was no longer swaying on the stool, I was fidgeting. I wanted to go to the loo. But I dared not go because if I left that room they might not let me back again and I just couldn't take a chance. I decided at all costs I would stick it out. I did my best for at least another half an hour and then I heard Aunt Liz call out, "Come along, Ralphie, it's time you went home." Alas her call had come too late – I had already wet my trousers.

Both Aunt Liz and Uncle Will are buried in Crewkerne and all except one of the family drifted away to other parts, the exception being their youngest daughter, my cousin Nellie. It was Nellie who upset the family more than any of the others because they had great plans for her and expected her to make a fine marriage. Who the intended bridegroom was supposed to be I don't know, but I do know their expectations did not fall beneath the possibilities of even an Earl or a Lord. She married a window cleaner! Nellie and I remained the closest of pals until the time of her death and I remember her with deep and loving affection.

Now for Aunt Nell. Beyond a doubt less financially blessed than any other member of the family (and to say that she had to make every penny count is putting it mildly) she brought up one of the biggest families of all the Reader clan. She was married to Asher Pattemore who worked at the local Co-op as a cobbler and his weekly salary was certainly nothing to write home about. Asher was a staunch Liberal and a signed photograph of Lloyd George hung in a prominent place in the main room of the home. When he attended the Baptist Church every Sunday it was God he worshipped, but when he was at home or at the Liberal Club, it was Lloyd George. There was never much love lost between Asher and Will Lye because of their different political views, but their two wives kept well above this.

Aunt Nell was far and away my favourite Aunt. I loved her. She was a very plump woman but no matter how big she was, her size could not compare with the great capacity of her heart. She was known to all her family as "Mam" and was accepted by each one of them as the boss and the boss she surely was. With only a few pounds coming in each week and every shilling having to be eked out, how she ever fed and clothed all those children is a miracle. I was often there for a meal and no plates have ever been as full as those Aunt Nell always managed to put on the table. She was not exactly a tidy soul, but this is excusable with all the work she had to do, and yet the speed with which she could clear a table after a meal can only be described as jet-propelled. Everything suddenly vanished and she didn't always care where it vanished to. Bread could disappear into the nearest chest-of-drawers where quite likely a pair of woollen bloomers were hiding and anything handy, from a bucket to an old empty tin, would find itself a receptacle for the remains of a stew or whatever left-overs there were. It was all done with such lightning speed that any caller suddenly walking in (as they frequently did) would find the room looking spick and span. Her youngest son, Bill, was my particular friend and I was very proud of him because he went to the Crewkerne Grammar School and this, to me, was the equivalent of being presented at Court. Bill had the quickest way of talking I have ever known and what's more the most incredible sense of humour. Even Ken Dodd could not outdo Bill when he got going and had he chosen the stage as a career he would have become one of our outstanding comedians. To this day he can still keep an audience in hysterics with his natural flow of hilarious chatter. He is irrepressible even at a wake.

I've had more kindness showered upon me by Aunt Nell than by all the rest of my relations put together (with one exception which I'll tell you about later), and when she got on the subject of our ancestors even Bill had to take a back seat. One of her favourite stories was of a long-gone relative who was a sheep-stealer and was sentenced to be hanged. On the day of the execution crowds gathered and walked beside him on his way to the gallows. Apparently some of them got too close to him and occasionally pushed him. He stood this for as long as he could and then suddenly stopped. He glared at the mob and in a loud voice shouted at them, "Stop your shoving, there's no hurry, they can't start 'til I get there." (The story has never been proved!)

My Aunt Nell made the best faggots of anyone in Crewkerne and she was a specialist in cleaning and cooking chitterlings. I won't go into details as to where chitterlings come from but they needed a lot of cleaning before they were put into the pot and in this cleaning she excelled. You don't see many chitterlings around these days, but I assure you if they had cost fifty pounds an ounce (instead of about three-pence a pound) they would have been put in the same class by the rich as caviar. Aunt Nell has passed on now but until the day she died she held her family together like an octopus and if what we believe in is true then the day she left us I'm certain Saint Peter was expecting her arrival and greeted her with the words, "Come on in Mam, He's waiting for you."

On my mother's side there is only one about whom I have a lot to say, with perhaps the exception of her mother, my Grandma. The brothers – Eli, Jim and Ted – I did not know very well. However, Ted used to visit us far more than the others and therefore I knew him best. He was a strong Salvationist and quite a character. His wife left him in preference for a young lodger, he got a divorce and married again, the second wife died and undiscouraged he looked around for a third. I joked to him about this when I knew he was 'hunting' and he solemnly quoted, "Ah my son, remember the Good Book says, 'Man can not live by bread alone' " so I presumed he was after more bread – and butter. One evening when I was playing in a revue at the Stoll Theatre in London, he came into my dressing room after the performance and with a glint in his eye told me he had a 'friend' outside the stage door who wanted to meet me. She wouldn't venture inside so I took my make-up off, dressed and went to meet the friend whom I was fully aware would be a lady and the next hoped-for 'Mrs. Ted.' I was right. She appeared to be in her fifties and was rather like an elderly edition of Dick Emery in his character of "Mavis." She acted like him too because when Uncle Ted said to her, "Dear, this is Ralph," she gave me a warming slosh on the chest which pushed me back to the wall and said, "Oh you are a cough-drop." I swear Dick, who was in the show, must have been watching and remembered! The lady outlived Ted.

There was one other brother, the youngest, and his name was Fred. To him I owe more than to any other person in the world. In 1914 he was called up for the Army and he rented a small cottage in Denton near Newhaven where he took his wife and small daughter. It was at this period that my school doctor suspected I had a touch of T.B. and decided I should stay away from school for a term and get away somewhere near the sea. Uncle Fred immediately suggested that I should live with his family in Sussex and there I went, never to go to school again. The events that followed changed the rest of my life. Rose Cottage became my new home and I became one of the family. From then on, Uncle Fred became my guardian and eventually I called him Pop and Pop he remained. His father-in-law, who also lived in Denton, was a greengrocer who had a round calling at houses in Seaford selling fruit and vegetables, and on this round I went three times a week. This kept me out in the open, getting plenty of sea air, and on days we were not travelling I helped in the allotments. Undoubtedly whatever was wrong with me was quickly put right and I became a very healthy boy. Naturally, I called my employer Grandad.

Every week he went into Brighton to the market to buy fresh supplies. This meant staying overnight, and it was on these occasions that he took me to the Brighton Hippodrome. For the first time I began to see something of the glamour of the stage. I watched with bulging eyes the variety stars of the day – Marie Lloyd, Vesta Tilley, George Robey, Jack Pleasants, and many of the Harry Day Revues starring Daisy Dormer, Dorothy Ward, Charlie Austin, Clarice Mayne and Ella Retford, to name but a few. The costumes of the chorus girls and the scenery and the lights all added up to a land of magic I could hardly believe existed. The Brighton Hippodrome became my wonderland and little did I dream then that one day I would not only be starring there but would produce and write my own shows and stay in the best hotels – a far cry from those early days when, after seeing a show, Grandad and I went back and slept in the stable with the horse. The war years passed and Uncle Fred came home from the Army and I remember I put on my Scout uniform to welcome him. As far back as I can remember, he never called me anything but 'son'. Perhaps this was due to the fact that my mother was his favourite sister whom he worshipped, but I was always 'son' and through all the years of my life I have used this title to thousands of boys who have been associated with me in every conceivable project. I don't believe any single boy I have known has not at some time been called by me, 'son' – and a very willing army of boys will confirm this.

I was fourteen when the war was ending and I became a telegraph messenger at the Newhaven Post Office. I had to work until ten o'clock every night and this sadly interfered with my Scouting life and with my particular interest in promoting concerts in the village. Then I had a great piece of luck. One night when I was delivering a telegram to the manager of the cement works in South Heighton (which was then a bomb disposal plant known as T.W.D.) I asked if there was a vacancy for an office boy. There was, and I got the job. The office was only a five minute walk from Rose Cottage so this suited me fine, and I really began in earnest to run the Scout Troop and, in addition to forming a football team, started seriously putting on shows. Eventually, the cement works reverted to its proper function and I was kept on, having graduated to junior clerk.

Life was good. Regular attendances at Church every Sunday, including my confirmation. I rose to the rank of Troop Leader in the Scouts and ran the Troop until our Scoutmaster returned from the war. Then came one of those incidents that change the lives of so many of us. A sister of Pop's wife came home for a holiday from America. She saw one or two of the shows I had put on and, although I had no knowledge of it at the time, she became very interested. Eventually she returned to New York, where she was a nurse, but she did not forget me. Also at this time a trade depression set in and it was decided to close the Newhaven cement works. The manager, a Mr. Beale, was transferred to the North of Ireland and he invited me to go with him. I jumped at the proposal and Pop agreed it would be a good thing for me. The very day I was due to leave for Ireland a letter came from my aunt in America telling me she would pay my fare and look after me if I would go to New York where, so she said, she knew some people connected with the stage and she thought they would be able to launch me on a theatrical career. It's not difficult to appreciate the position I found myself in. More than anything I longed to be a performer and here seemed the great opportunity. On the other hand I had promised to go to Ireland the very next day, so after much thinking and much talk with the family it was agreed that I had to keep faith with Mr. Beale. So, on April 1st to Ireland I went after writing to my aunt in the States, thanking her but explaining the position. I was to leave Euston for Stranraer on the Monday night, so I got to London in time to see the matinee at the Palladium of a spectacular revue called *Rockets.* Watching the performers in that show brought lump after lump in my throat when I realised that, had I taken up the American offer, one day I might have even appeared on that very stage. (One day I did – not only for a day but in variety and in four Royal Command Performances, but that's another part of the story).

So now, after giving you the background of my family and the start of my leaving home to go to Ireland, let me tell one or two things about what became the happiest time of my life – seven months in Magheramorne, County Antrim, Northern Ireland, and how I became adopted as the ninth son of the Doherty family.

3

Ireland and the Dohertys

I came out of the Palladium after the matinee of *Rockets* and made my way to Euston Station. I had a couple of hours to wait before train time so I went into the refreshment room for a cup of tea and a sandwich. Station sandwiches haven't changed through the years and this particular one had nearly as many curves on it as the girls in the show I had just seen. The tea too was hardly worthy of the name but I managed quite well by dunking the sandwich into the liquid. This did not go un-noticed by a kind man sitting next to me who smiled and said, "You having trouble too, mate?" However, I had a precious possession in my pocket, and this I pulled out and read through half-a-dozen times. It was the programme of *Rockets*. Nearly every line of that show came back to me and to this day I remember the names of the cast – Charlie Austin, Lorna and Toots Pounds, Ivor Vintor and Freddy Forbes. I can still hear little Ivor Vintor repeatedly saying, "I want to see the giraffe."

Then came the moment when I was to meet Mr. Beale on the platform. It was an all-night journey and he had kindly paid for a cushion to help me sleep. He was travelling first class, I was travelling third. There were only two of us in my carriage so we were able to put our feet up, and after an hour or so I fell asleep. Before doing so I watched the houses of London change to open fields and once again my mind went back to the Palladium. I must have dozed off still dreaming of that show because suddenly the man on the opposite seat said to me, "You want to *WHAT*?" "Pardon?" I replied. "You said you wanted to see the giraffe" and giving me a peculiar look he went on, "Well don't bring it in here." I decided then and there that I should have to change my trend of thought in case the man called for the guard, so I began to think of what Ireland would be like, whether I would find it easy to settle down, what my lodgings would be like and whether they kept pigs in the house. The idea of seeing pigs took my mind away from the giraffe. The rhythm of the train must have done the trick because in a few more moments I fell asleep. When I awoke, the train was slowing down and I knew we were reaching the end of the first part of the journey.

It was very early in the morning when the train arrived at Stranraer and we embarked on the ferry and went straight down to breakfast. This was quite an experience for me, though the smell of fried bacon was a little too much to give me an appetite – maybe because it was coupled with a strong smell of kippers – so all I ate was a few slices of toast. Then we set sail and I went on deck to find the sun coming up and deciding to make it a very bright day.

It was a beautiful sight as we passed through the loch and headed towards the open water, and for once the Irish Sea was like the proverbial mill pond. I ran all over the ship, going from side to side, filled with excitement, for to me this was a genuine adventure. It seemed I was sailing away to a new world with a new life opening up before me. I tried to think of how I would explain it all when I wrote my first letter home. All my pals in the Troop would be so envious when I sent them cards which I bought on the ship and I went below to write one or two straight away. Then Mr. Beale found me and beckoned to me to follow him up on deck. He put his arm on my shoulder and said, "Well, there it is." I looked and I said nothing. I just looked.

I had my first sight of Ireland when we were several miles out of Larne, and the view was one to remember. Such green fields everywhere and all over the hills for miles and miles were small white-washed cottages almost shining in the sun. Straight ahead of us and getting closer and closer was Larne Harbour. It was a scene I remember to this day. When the boat docked we came ashore where a car was waiting for us, and Mr. Beale and his wife took me through one or two typical little villages until we reached Magheramorne. Magheramorne is a small village in two distinct parts, one on the lower road and the other high up on a hill. (The cement works were situated on the lower road). Up on the high road there was a wonderful view of Larne Harbour and the Irish Sea which immediately seemed to be the barrier between me and home; but with such different surroundings I was bound to feel a certain excitement which went a long way towards keeping my spirits up, and nothing helped this more than being taken to No. 26, Quintons Row, to meet Mrs. McConnell, with whom I was to stay. The welcome I had was so warm and genuine, and her three young daughters and her son Tom made it obvious that they intended to make me feel at home. They laid on the biggest breakfast I've ever seen and I ate the lot. They all sat round the table in the little room and chatted and laughed with me and kept filling my plate the moment they saw an empty space. And they drank tea – gallons it seemed to me – and they expected me to do the same. When the meal was finished I had a wash and was then taken down to the lower road to the cement works to meet my future colleagues. I was given the rest of the day off.

I walked back to Mrs. McConnell's up the Ballyleg Road, a very long and steep climb it is too, and then I sat down to write a letter home. It was far from easy, because I had never been away from home before, and even at seventeen it is not difficult to become homesick and I *was* beginning to feel a trifle that way. Tea-time came and once again the table was filled, this time with every sort of bread and cakes and jams, so I knew that whatever else overtook me in Ireland, hunger never would.

That evening, there was a concert to be held in a neighbouring village (Ballycarry) and Mrs. McConnell thought I might like to go. I jumped at the idea. It was only three miles, so we were to walk each way. Now this was the time of the 'trouble' (and I bet you've heard that before) but the trouble meant nothing to me so off we went in high spirits to see the performance.

Unfortunately, it was the kind of evening we hadn't expected. The concert had only been going for about an hour when there was a commotion at the back of the hall. It became louder and then chairs began to fly. Shouts followed and within minutes the place was in an uproar. Tom McConnell grabbed my hand and said, *"Out!"* We dared not try to get through the fighting crowd at the rear of the hall so we jumped over the stage and escaped by the back door. Then we ran, but only for about ten minutes. There was a curfew on at the time and it appears we were over-time so when we heard the approach of the armoured cars, we all flung ourselves into a ditch until they had passed. Then we ran the rest of the way home. I was not amused! Mrs. McConnell was in her nightdress when we arrived. We had to relate all that had happened to us and I remember how she laughed and said, "Don't worry, Mr. Reader, you'll get used to it." I didn't think I would and in any case that night I made up my mind that I wouldn't even try to. So the very next morning, before going to work, I wrote to my aunt in America saying that if her offer still held good I would accept it. I posted the letter on my way to work next morning. That night, as I finished my dinner, there was a knock on the door of the cottage. Some boys were there and they asked me if I would like to come with them and play football. They introduced themselves to me as 'The Dohertys'. If I had met those boys one day earlier I would never have gone to America, so what my future would have been is difficult to imagine. With my lack of education I could never have risen to any important post in the cement works and I could have looked forward only to a very humble and perhaps mundane career, but the letter was already on its way to the United States of America.

The Dohertys were sons of the Minister of Magheramorne, and the Rev. Doherty and his wife had eight, the eldest a year older than me, the next the same age and the remainder each one year younger. Before the week was out we were brothers in every sense of the word except by birth. I was taken to the Manse to meet Mr. and Mrs. Doherty and from that moment I knew I belonged to them.

I remember the nights we played tennis until it was so dark we couldn't see even the net, let alone the ball. But it was fun. The only competition I have ever won was in Magheramorne at tennis. The prize was a clock which I took back with me to Rose Cottage. Although it kept good time, it had the loudest tick of any clock I have ever heard, and even to this day, when I hear a hundred Guardsmen marching down the steps of the Albert Hall, I think they make much less noise than that clock did. It didn't merely keep *me* awake, it even troubled the people next door!

Football too took up an important part of our free time, and when we weren't playing games we just sat by the little bridge with a rolling stream running along beneath it and talked until the twilight turned to darkness. It never mattered what we talked about, we just talked, and when we ran out of conversation we all sat there together, perfectly contented. I guess that was as good an example as any of what friendship really means.

I began to know everyone in the village and I fell in love with the most wonderful girl I have ever known – Anne Jane Blair. No girl before or since has meant so much to me. She died whilst I was in America.

The seven months I spent in Magheramorne were the

glory days of my youth and some part of me will always be wherever the Dohertys are. Years later, when one of the shows that I had produced played at the Belfast Opera House, the papers came out with the headline, "The 9th Doherty son comes home." The highest compliment I have ever had came from the Rev. Doherty, who went on the stage at the last concert I did before I left – it was in the old recreation hall at the cement works – and said, "If Reader hadn't been an Englishman I would have liked him to be an Ulsterman." If I have been half as good a man as the Rev. Doherty I have not done too badly.

But those gloriously happy days were speeding by, each one bringing me nearer to the time when I had to leave. My aunt in America had writen back to say "Come", and I felt that this time I could not refuse so I replied saying that I would go. I told the boys that same night. It wasn't a happy evening, but we were all young and youth has a strange way of getting over things. Even so, I knew that the day I left would be the saddest day of my life and it certainly was.

Naturally the Friday night before my departure the following day I spent with Anne. It was one of those evenings which will always linger in my memory. Neither of us dreamed it would be our very last night together. People often laugh at what they call puppy love but few understand how deep and sincere such love can be. Young love is often the sweetest of all emotions and at seventeen it can probe and discover perfection. Anne's father was a very strict man and he did not approve of his youngest daughter having a boy-friend, but with the aid of her sister, Lizzie, she was smuggled out of the house the moment Mr. Blair went to bed. Luckily he retired early as he rose at the crack of dawn each morning to attend to his farm. I sat on the bank by the roadside and waited about an hour before Anne appeared and for the next couple of hours there were no other people in the world, only the two of us. It was about ten o'clock when we said goodbye. I kissed her again and watched her walk away toward her house. She turned and waved. I didn't. Somehow I couldn't because I knew it would be years before I could be with her again, and long after she had gone inside and closed the door I still remained there, little dreaming, thank God, that when I *did* see her again some seven years later she would be lying in a bed in a shed in the garden dying of consumption. I loved and I lost and because I was never prepared to accept a second-best, my young love has never grown old. Then I walked down to the Manse where I knew the boys would be waiting for me and we talked and talked until well after midnight. Finally, they walked with me back to Mrs. McConnell, her three girls and Tom were still up and we weren't a very happy crowd, but the die was cast so we soon said goodnight and I went to bed. My last thoughts that night were of what I knew I should be leaving behind me the next day.

I awoke early on the Saturday morning and packed my things. Several of the neighbours came in to wish me good luck and brought me little presents. Long before I wanted it to, the day passed and it was time to head for Larne Harbour where the ship was waiting. John, Bill, Leslie, R.G., Jim, Hubert, Matt and another of our mates, Nelson Craigh, came to see me off. I went on board and stood at the rail of the boat with a very heavy heart. We joked a bit and shouted the usual cracks one does on these occasions and then the siren sounded, ropes were thrown over and the boat began to move. There was not a smile on any face and not a word was spoken – nobody even waved. As the gap between the boat and the dock became wider I felt like jumping off and then, as it drew further away, I looked up away across to the hill where Quinton Cottages stood and there was Mrs. McConnell, Tom and the girls waving a large white table-cloth. It was their way of bidding me goodbye. I'm no hero and long before the quayside and the figures of the boys still standing there disappeared I went down below deck and burst into tears. It was the end of seven months – just seven short months – but because of the Dohertys, those months were the most wonderful of my life.

But now it was back to Rose Cottage, the visits to the American Embassy to get permits and to the Passport Office to obtain my passport. I was to sail from Southampton on the *Homeric* and within three weeks I was packed and ready to bid Denton goodbye. I didn't get a very memorable send-off as nobody came to the station to see me board the train at Newhaven. I carried my own bags from Denton and I remember just one of the villagers who happened to be in her garden saw me and waved. Pop was the only one who would have been with me but he couldn't get away from work, so I stood on the platform waiting for the train, alone and feeling somewhat disappointed. In came the train and in I got, put my luggage on the rack, sat down, and watched the train gather speed as it left the familiar spots I knew so well. One of the passengers in the carriage noticed my bags and asked me if I were going on a holiday. I shook my head because somehow I just couldn't speak. The journey to Southampton didn't take long and I had to stay there overnight as the ship did not leave until early next morning so they booked me into the dormitory of an hotel for the night. I managed to find a small theatre where a touring revue was playing and I went in to see it. I wished I hadn't as it was one of the sorriest affairs I have ever seen. It was so sad looking and there were so few people in the audience that I began to wonder if this was the sort of thing I was letting myself in for. I became so depressed that I left long before it was over and walked back to the hotel feeling as sorry for those poor performers as I was then feeling for myself. Was that going to be my fate? Thank God it wasn't.

I had a good night's sleep and woke early next morning filled with the excitement of expectation. I went down to the ship, sporting myself a taxi, and as I was paying the driver I looked up and saw the *Homeric*! I knew it would be a big ship, but anything like the size of this enormous vessel was beyond my wildest dreams. It seemed to rise higher than Big Ben and its length looked longer than the walk from Rose Cottage to Newhaven Station. Once aboard I felt I had walked into a palace. I had an inside second class cabin which I shared with a young American. About the first thing I asked him was "Who is your most famous comedian?" He quickly replied, "Al Jolson." Now I'd never heard of Al Jolson and I knew he'd never been to the Brighton Hippodrome so I was convinced he couldn't be any good. I didn't even see the ship leave the dock and when I went up on deck Southampton was behind me. I stared at the vanishing English coast and then looked out to sea and I remember I said out loud to myself, "America, here I come!"

4

I arrive in New York

Trying to describe my feelings as I sailed up the Hudson River in the early morning of that great day when I arrived in New York takes some doing. Steaming slowly by the Statue of Liberty is quite an experience, but even that is dwarfed by the first sight of the skyline of New York. It dazzles your eyes and hits your mind with the power of an explosion, and the nearer the ship slides into port the higher the buildings appear to tower, higher and higher toward the heavens and seemingly getting there. I looked, and felt stunned. My heart was thumping like the pistons of the ship's engines. I thought I was dreaming, but I suddenly awoke as I saw my aunt waving to me in the crowd waiting for the ship's arrival. I pushed and shoved my way with the crowd stampeding down the gangway and rushed towards her.

After collecting my luggage she hailed a taxi and we drove to 217, 76th Street, 3rd Avenue, where I was to lodge with a darling old German lady named Mrs. Litz. What a great friend she turned out to be, although I didn't know then just how much I would be needing that friendship. Nor how often! We sat down in the kitchen to a hearty meal and all the time my aunt was questioning me about the folk at home. I spent the afternoon unpacking, with my aunt taking stock of what clothes I possessed and noting several items I would be needing. Later that evening she decided it was time I was taken to see Broadway. Broadway, the greatest theatre-land in the world, and the world I had come to conquer. We took the subway and arrived at Times Square, the centre of all that New York stands for.

Of all the sights I have seen in the many parts of the world I visited during the years that followed, nothing can compare with the magic of Times Square at night. A million lights flickered everywhere – the gigantic Wrigley Chewing Gum sign, the blazing colours advertising the shows: The Palace Theatre where the Duncan Sisters, Elsie Janis, Nora Bayes and Eddy Leonard were appearing; the Ziegfield Follies with Eddie Cantor, Will Rogers, Gallagher and Sheen; Trini starring at the Winter Garden and Fred Stone at the Globe. Hundreds of taxi cabs were hooting their way in all directions and going to and from the subways were thousands and thousands of people, all of them in a hurry. Gripping my aunt's hand for safety I just stared, completely bewitched. Broadway, the longest street with the shortest memory. 42nd Street with live theatres cramming each side of the road, 7th Avenue bulging with the crowds crushing each other as they filled every inch of its length. Police blowing whistles to re-start traffic as it halted at the lights. And it was all for real.

We stood there for nearly an hour and then my aunt took me to the Hippodrome where we were to see my first American show. It was called *Better Times* but I can't remember much about it because my mind was still hypnotised by what I had seen when I was standing in Times Square. After the performance we walked back there again and it seemed to be even more crowded than before as people poured out of the cinemas and theatres to make their way home. And that was where we headed for too. Mrs. Litz had supper ready for us, but I couldn't eat a thing. Tomorrow was to be the start of my new life, as my aunt had arranged for me to meet her theatrical friend who was going to help me embark upon my stage career. It took me a long time to get to sleep that night because I'd seen too much and tomorrow was going to be a new beginning for me. It also turned out to be my first bitter awakening.

At ten o'clock next morning my aunt took me to a sleazy agent's office where I met a Mr. Carrero – he was her friend who had 'influence' and would steer me toward my future. Mr. Carrero turned out to be nothing more than a dresser to a fairly well-known character actor who was out of work, and so was Mr. Carrero! However, we chatted and then he told me he would take me around to some of his influential friends who were agents and would find me a job. Each office we went to seemed cheaper than the previous one and each agent asked me, "What have you done?" Naturally, I lied. I told them the various shows I had been appearing in, omitting of course to say that they were performed in that old dis-used chapel in South Heighton, but even the lowest type of agent can spot an amateur who had never been on the stage in his life. They all took my address and said, "You will be hearing from us." I never did! However, I had to live, so the only possible thing to do was to find some other job, and I was eventually taken on by the Onyx Hosiery Company as a ledger clerk.

The Onyx was a very big firm and I worked in one of those enormous offices containing dozens of desks, each with a telephone which rang continuously and made me feel I was in bedlam. I had to clock on each morning at eight o'clock and finished at five. I ate my lunch at the Automat and my main meal was with Mrs. Litz back home at No. 217. Each evening I went to Broadway and spent every cent I had seeing shows and various films, then took the long walk home to save the subway or tram fare. One night I saw a placard which announced that Al Jolson was returning to the Winter Garden for a period of four weeks. This show I was determined to see. Jolson's name had constantly been mentioned by the people in the office where I was working and the more they raved about him the less important he became to me – in fact I began to loathe any mention of him. It so happened that the only opportunity I had to see his show was on the final Saturday of his engagement and I went to see the matinée. Imagine my disgust when I arrived at the theatre to see a notice outside saying, "There will be no performance this afternoon as Mr. Jolson is taking the entire Company to the races." I was infuriated – to cancel a show was something I could not believe possible. Nevertheless I did buy a ticket for his final show that night. I went into the Winter Garden with almost hatred in my heart. "Who *is* this man who can take the afternoon off to go the races?" I sat in the gallery and waited for his appearance. The show was a musical comedy and he did not appear until about twenty minutes after the show had commenced. The house broke into tumultuous applause as soon as he entered. Everybody was cheering and clapping. He hadn't even opened his mouth but not a soul in that theatre was applauding louder than I was. He sang "California here I come," told a few jokes and then went into more numbers. I yelled for more. Inexperienced indeed I was, but I knew I was watching the greatest performer in the world and to this day that is how I rate him. After the performance I couldn't go home. I walked and walked through Central Park (something one dare not do today) until well after mid-night and all I could see was this great sensational man singing not to the audience but only to *me*.

His power and incredible genius had knocked me sideways. The black face, the white gloves, the dynamic personality and those flashing magic eyes swept me into a state of hypnotism such that I have known only once in my life, on that never-to-be forgotten night. I got home and tried to sleep but found it impossible. Next morning I went back to the Winter Garden and stood opposite the stage door where they were taking out the scenery. All I could think of was that those men carting out the props had actually known him, probably spoken to him and had been *with* him. It still seems impossible to me that one day *I* worked with him at that very theatre, and for over two years. If I appear to have exaggerated in telling you of the first impression I had of Al Jolson, let me assure you I have in fact under-estimated the effect he had on me.

About a week later, the Mr. Carerro I mentioned earlier rang me to say that he could get me an audition at a movie theatre which put on trial acts before the feature film. It was at Foxes Audobon way up on 168th Street. I leapt at the chance. It meant getting away from the office for a day, so I played sick. I was to do two appearances, one in the afternoon and again in the evening. Unfortunately I secretly told a girl who had been kind to me about this and she passed the news on to some of the others in the office and they decided to come along and see me on the night show. I hired a tuxedo (dinner jacket) and chose for my act three English songs, which was damnation to start with. One of these was a song some of you may remember, "All the girls are busy knitting jumpers." Now they don't refer to jumpers as such in the States, they call them sweaters, so whilst I was wading through this song, the audience at the afternoon performance were puzzled as to why any girl should be knitting fleas. They were also puzzled as to why I had been allowed to perform. I came off with the mildest sympathetic applause and sneaked away to my dressing room. One of the assistant stage managers was there before me and all he said was, "Pack your things, bud, you're through." I tried to raise a grin and said, "I was a flop, wasn't I?" Not a muscle moved on his face as he replied, "We don't call that a flop, son, we call it a diabolical catastrophe." I was glad he closed the door quickly. When the people from the office came to see me that evening, they didn't, and whatever they assumed was perfectly correct.

It was a tragic experience. I had hired the tuxedo but the fact that I needed studs and cuff-links hadn't occurred to me so, long before I got through my first song, my cuffs were down to my finger nails and I'm still not sure what happened to my collar. Luckily the bow tie held fairly firm and this helped, but long before I finished my "turn" one side of the collar was clipping my ear. Not a word was said to me by any of my colleagues at the office the next day, but I did notice my girl-friend was trying to be exceedingly kind and kindness was something I sorely needed. I didn't get it from anyone else. Four days later a phone call came to me in the office and to my surprise and elation a man's voice told me that he had seen my act and that if I would go immediately to the Palace Theatre Building, a Mr. Pat Hastings was waiting for me to sign a 52 week contract with the Keith Circuit. Now the Keith Circuit was the biggest vaudeville group in America, so you can imagine what joy that telephone message meant to me. I grabbed a telephone and rang my aunt who was working in New Jersey. I talked loudly as I wanted all those around me to know the wonderful news and that I *wasn't* the flop they imagined me to be. In fact, I smiled at them rather sarcastically. It was about five o'clock on a winter's day and snow was everywhere (except in my heart). I raced out of the office, boarded a tram, which luckily cost only five cents for any length of journey, and I got out at Times Square. Then I walked to the Palace Theatre Building. It wasn't far, but far enough for me to get wet through. My hat had blown off but who cared? I certainly didn't. The snow was rolling down but I brushed off as much as I could and went into the elevator and up to the eleventh floor to find the office of Mr. Pat Hastings. I couldn't find it, simply because there was no Mr. Hastings and there had been no phone call from that building. I went to floor after floor with panic growing with each step I took. No office was open, not a light anywhere except in the passages. I was exhausted and leaned up against a wall when the truth suddenly dawned on me. That phone call had been a joke by one of the men in the Onyx Hosiery Company!

I need hardly tell you how I felt because I am sure your imagination will do just that. I walked all the way back to Mrs. Litz and by this time even my underwear was soaked through and my shoes were squelching melted snow with each step I took. There was an old shop which sold second-hand books at the corner of 76th Street and as I passed it I noticed one of the books had fallen from the shelf and was lying on the floor of the window. For some unknown reason I stopped to look at the book. Its title was, *The Road to Understanding.* I crept into the house and, thank God, Mrs. Litz was out. I went into my bedroom and without even taking off my drenched overcoat I sat in an old armchair and wept.

Not a word was said next day at the office, but about three weeks later, as I was coming down in the elevator after finishing work, a tall young man came up to me and said, "I was the guy who made that phone call." I punched him right in the face. He didn't retaliate but quietly said, "Ralph, I deserved that" and he put out his hand. I shook it.

Two days later I was reading a copy of *Variety,* the great theatrical weekly which is read by everyone in the profession, when I came across a small advertisement which stated, "Do you need stage coaching? Ring, 02-79943, The Studio at 249, West 52nd Street." I did, and went for an interview. There are numerous expensive drama schools but not one of these can compare either in what they taught or how they taught with this little Studio where I eventually enrolled. It was run by a Mr. Hallett and a Miss François, and to them I owe so much. They took me in at a reduced rate, taught me elocution and insisted that I learned to dance. Dancing was something I had never thought about nor wanted to do, but they made me. Within four months I had learned more than I ever dreamed a performer had to know. The days were long, because after finishing at the Onyx at five o'clock I went home for a meal and then down to the Studio and worked until midnight for six nights a week and all day on Sundays. Then came the moment when Mr. Hallett thought I was good enough to go into a small new vaudeville act. It was only a small part but he insisted it would be experience. So I left the Onyx and joined this new act. It lasted three days.

"Don't be discouraged" Miss François told me, "Get another job until something else turns up." I spent the next two months opening crates at Lord and Taylor's, one of the biggest department stores in New York, and then along came another opportunity. A vaudeville act again, but this one lasted an entire week. By now my dancing was greatly improving and I began to enjoy it, but, being out of work, I had to find other employment. This time I found myself in the office of the Manhatten Shirt Company on Madison Avenue (which turned out to be my last job outside show business). The tide was beginning to turn, and one morning Miss François rang me and told me to report at the Court Theatre where they were auditioning chorus boys for a new musical comedy which would go on tour and then come to Broadway. During the following lunch hour along I went to the Court Theatre, and there, standing on the stage, was another young chap of my own age. He too was there for an audition but every one had gone to lunch and we hunted round to try to find the dance director, who happened to be having his lunch (and a drink) in one of the dressing rooms. He came down on the stage and tried us out with various steps. As a result, we both got a job. The other boy and I became firm friends (and still are) and he eventually turned out to be one of the brightest stars in musical films for Paramount. His name was Jack Oakie. We went over to the nearest drug store and bought a coke and then by a strange coincidence we found we were both working at the same place.

Sharlee was the name of the musical and we rehearsed for

four weeks and then opened on the road making the usual changes in routines etc. Oakie and I 'digged' together. We had two other special pals in that chorus, a Joe Hughes and a chap we called "Cowboy." We made a fine quartette and the tour was loaded with laughs although the work, with the constant change of dance routines and learning new steps, made every waking hour an endurance test. But it was fun. We opened three weeks later at Dalys Theatre in New York and on the opening night I got my notice! Nobody could ever find out why, but the two weeks' notice came just the same. As it happened, things could not have worked out better, because the next day I went to the Chorus Equity to find out if there were any other shows in rehearsal. I was lucky as they sent me to the roof of the Century Theatre on 59th Street to try out for a Mr. Jack Mason, who was the dance director of a new big Shubert musical. On my way up there I decided it might sound more important if I told them that I was sent by the Shubert Office instead of the Chorus Equity (remember I was very ignorant in those days). I had heard the other chorus boys in *Sharlee* talking of a Miss Cummings (that's not the real name) who always interviewed boys for the Shubert choruses, so when I reached the Century rehearsal rooms and Mr. Mason asked who had sent me I simply lied and said "Miss Cummings." Now Mr. Mason was just about the toughest character one could ever meet and he glared at me and said, "WHO?" I repeated, "Miss Cummings." He gave me a look that withered me and said, "Come outside." Then he gave me a lecture using words that even the toughest sergeant-major had never heard of and finally said, "You're a god-damned limey and you're lying like hell, but I've just come back from England (he had been working for C.B. Cochran producing *Little Nelly Kelly*) and they gave me the time of my life so you're in – but don't you ever say "Miss Cummings" again – he's a MAN." I raced back to the theatre that night to tell the boys of my good fortune and discovered they had just been informed the show we were in was due to close. It was a flop and was finishing on the same night as my notice would have expired. Next day I spoke to Jack Mason and got Joe, "Cowboy" and Oakie in the show with me. How's that for luck?

Our new show was called *Innocent Eyes* and starred that great Parisian artiste, Mistinguett. We toured for nine weeks and then returned to open at the Winter Garden. Yes, the Winter Garden where I had first seen Jolson. What a chorus we had in that show. Jack Oakie, Nancy Carrol, Joan Crawford, George Raft and several others who were to make their names in pictures. The show was a tremendous success and played for months. Each morning we used to go to the theatre and practise steps to improve our dancing. Competition was tremendous in those days (I suppose it's the same today) and it was up to every chorus boy and girl to keep absolutely fit and ready for whenever the next audition might turn up.

My first experience of "La Grande Passion" happened round about this time and it was worthy of an "X" Certificate.

With the show we had a wardrobe mistress who stood about six feet tall, weighed somewhere around fourteen stone and had red bobbed hair. (It wasn't its real colour but apparently had been chosen for its significance). She developed a weakness, and unfortunately that weakness was for me. Strange though it may seem I was the last person to catch on to this, but it should have been obvious by the number of clean collars and shirts I was getting —whereas the other chorus-boys had to make theirs last the entire week.

One night, being slower to change than usual, I was very nearly the last one to leave the theatre. The assistant wardrobe mistress on her way out came to our dressing-room and said to me, "Will you take your soiled shirt up to Mrs. "W" as she's sending them out first thing in the morning." Away she went and I dutifully collected my shirt and took it upstairs to the wardrobe.

As I got inside, a deft move closed the door behind me and locked it. The key hung from a bunch dangling from the waist of a woman jailer. I put my linen on the end table and turned to face the wardrobe mistress! There she stood, arms akimbo, smiling broadly and confidentially. For an instant I suspected nothing, but then she said, "English, kiss me!" I froze.

Even with my inexperience, one always knows when a woman means business and, brother, that woman meant business. She was a good thirty years older than I was, but there was a complete absence of any maternal feeling in her demand. I countered with a slick piece of repartee. I said, "What for?" She opened the scoring by replying "I'll show ya," and with one move rushed me. I was encircled by two iron bars of thick-armed muscle which crushed the breath out of me and made my eyes stand out three inches from the rest of my face. She kissed me and I felt as though I were under water, except that I couldn't struggle. I was petrified, for fear told me this was only the trailer.

I felt as though I were going to collapse when she broke away from my face. I felt a clang which I believed had broken my neck, but all she had done was to push my head on to her shoulder. She released one arm to reach for an open gin bottle standing ripe and ready on the table. I heard a guzzle, then a wooden thud as the bottle was replaced, and felt another jerk as her fist flicked my head back to the required position for an encore. I knew I had to make an effort, so I tried to struggle, but the woman took this for encouragement and gleefully murmured, "Atta boy!" What would have happened no one will ever know, for at that very moment, just as in the movies, a loud knock sounded on the door and a tough man's voice demanded, "You still there, Lil?" A thick podgy hand smothered my mouth to prevent me from murmuring and she hissed in my ear, "Shh, it's Bert." (He was her husband). Stark fear covered me and I waited for three bullets to blow the lock off the door and another three to finish me off. But no. Bert decided she had gone home and I heard him thumping his way down the stairs. Without a word, Lil took my hand, pulled me across the long dressing-room toward a window which she opened, and there was a fire-escape. Still holding my hand, she led me down, down, down until we reached street level and I found the pavement of 7th Avenue solidly under my feet. Before I realised it she had stuffed a dollar bill into my hand. "See you at the matinée," she said and, strutting off towards Times Square, left me motionless and feeling as though I had just taken a plunge in frozen waters.

Then life returned and I rushed toward an on-coming trolley, paid my nickel and sat down facing a tough-looking New Yorker who grinned at me. I sheepishly returned the grin and then with a wink he said, "She sure must have been some girl, Bud." I nodded weakly, wondering how he could have known. At 76th Street as I got off, the conductor said to me, "Did it cost you much?" I didn't reply but ran as fast as I could to 217. As I entered the kitchen, Mrs. Litz took one look at me and said, "So you've started, aye?" I froze. Already there must have been headlines in the papers, news-lights blazing my experience to the reading crowds in the Square and maybe even the radio putting out flashes of my downfall. But as I glanced in the mirror my face told me everything, for it was smothered and smeared by bright red lipstick. I never again went up to that wardrobe-room alone, but I still have the dollar bill even to this day.

During this period I was still attending The Studio at least three times a week and on various Sundays I would work in a charity show they were staging just for the experience. I cannot think of a more important word than "experience" and Mr. Hallett and Miss François decided I needed just that, so I left the chorus of *Innocent Eyes* to join a small stock company which was due to tour small towns in Canada. The money was half what I was getting in the Winter Garden Show but I had such faith in the judgement of these two dear people that I agreed to do as they suggested.

There were only nine of us in the cast of the Taylor McCauliffe Stock Company, and we played only such melodramas as were out of copyright. *Ten nights in a Bar Room, The Minister's Sweetheart* and *Over the Hill to the Poorhouse* were but three of our repertoire. What's more, after each act we had to come in front of the house tabs and do a song and dance as the locals we were playing to didn't like waiting whilst the next scene was set. I remember in *Ten nights in a Bar Room* I was killed at the end of the Second Act and quickly revived to leap in front of the tabs and sing a couple of songs and do a dance. Business wasn't good, in fact it was bad right from the beginning of the tour and got steadily worse. Wages couldn't be paid, but optimistically we hoped and hoped that the next town would be better. It never was. We had to find the cheapest digs, and this wasn't easy, for in those days actors were not considered exactly trustworthy people. In fact there was a saying going around, "Take in your washing missus, actors are coming." I never left one of my digs without paying but I came very close to it once and I think the story is worth telling.

It was in a place called River Hebet. I was staying for three days with two very sweet old ladies: in their living room they had a small harmonium which I often played. The fact that I could play hymns seemed to please them mightily, and we had some happy times together during that short stay, singing old favourites together. They would never come to the show. It somehow did not fit in with their scheme of things; but they were very sympathetic.

Our business during these three days was terrible and it was obvious that by the end of the week there would be no money to come to us at all. We were due to leave on the Sunday afternoon and I knew that sooner or later I should have to tell them that I could not pay for my lodgings. The three of us went to Church that Sunday morning and then after lunch I went up to my room to decide how I could break the news to them. It had to be done, so with fear in my heart I descended the stairs and knocked at the door of their room.

They were sitting one each side of the fireplace. It was no good beating about the bush, so I came straight to the point: "I've come about my rent." One of the dear souls smiled at me and said, "Now, Mr. Reader, my sister and I have just been talking about you. You have given us so much pleasure since you have been here that we would like you to do something more for us. Please remember us kindly on your travels, and we want you to be our guest. We couldn't possibly accept anything from you, and whenever you come back again there will always be a home for you."

Well, I *have* remembered them – how could I forget? – and I thank them always for helping me out of that awful moment.

The obvious ending came and we found ourselves stranded. We first had to make our way back to Boston and to do so we gave concerts in any old hall we could find and on two occasions even walked to the next town carrying our grips and the bits and pieces we needed for a performance. But we reached Boston after an exhausting three to four weeks and then the next goal was to get to New York. We were lucky. A lorry driver was returning to the city and he gave us a lift all the way, so at long last we were "home" again and my first port of call was The Studio. There was a small intimate revue rehearsing there and Miss François got me the job of producing the dances for the show and also of playing various parts. Without doubt, this was the beginning of all that started me on the upward way.

The show was called *Bad Habits* and it opened at the Greenwich Village Theatre, downtown New York. We got bad notices, but the show ran for several weeks. The dance routines I had staged went well and one particular number *Now did ya?* was one of the hits of the performance. We were a very young Company and every night various agents would be out front looking for whatever talent might be worth taking a chance on. It was on one of these nights that a note came back to me from someone sitting out front which read, "I'd like to see you after the performance." It was signed, "Gene Macgregor." Macgregor was attached to one of the biggest agencies on Broadway and was therefore a very important man, and the fact that he wanted to see me was flattering to say the least. He came back after the Finale and invited me to have supper with him. Gene was a middle-aged man with great charm and when we got to the coffee stage he began to talk business. It wasn't all compliments he paid me that night. He told me I hadn't much of a voice; I needed to pay a lot more attention to my timing of lines; and I badly needed experience. The things he did enthuse about were my own personal dancing and the way I staged the numbers in the show. "You need handling, Ralph, and you need direction. I know you've done your stint in the chorus and I'm told you have played in some honkey-tonk dramatic junk in Canada, but your aim must be Broadway and I believe you can get there if you can take advice and, above all, *LISTEN*. You're very young and that's in your favour *IF* you can keep your head and allow someone to guide you." I agreed with him and said I understood exactly what he meant, "But," I went on, "Who guides me?" He put out his hand and said, "I will if you give me your word to do exactly as I say and rely on me entirely." I had only just met Gene but there was something about him that 'got' me. From then on it was just that and because of his judgement, his foresight and his devotion, all that came to me from that night onwards belongs to Gene Macgregor.

He started by getting me engagements to stage small night club shows; he made me play in drab second-hand dumps in Brooklyn, Atlantic City, Harlem and in dives where the customers not merely looked as though they had just escaped from jail – some of them had. He sat through every performance and at times I nearly lost heart. If this is the road to Broadway, I thought, then somehow we've taken the wrong turning. It was then he talked to me. Halfway through the night he would sit on my bed and use the word 'experience' until I got sick of it. Every time I tried to open my mouth to speak he'd keep ahead of me and just talk on. And every time I weakened and in order to get some sleep I'd say, "Alright Gene, you win." And win he did – for me.

The first decent job he got me was to stage the dance routines for a major touring show, called *Cynthia,* which opened in Philadelphia. This was followed by another touring show, *Miss Happiness,* and although neither show played in New York the numerous kind remarks the reviewers made about the dances were apparently spotted by several major show promoters, and were brought to the attention of such firms as the Shuberts, Ziegfield, Dillingham and Earl Carrol (probably by Gene). So, although these two shows were playing outside the Big White Way, they were certainly not unheard of. At least, the dance producer wasn't!

My aunt, Gene and I went to supper one night at a fashionable restaurant to celebrate my twenty-second birthday. That party wasn't quite as happy as it should have been. Gene and I had a bit of a row. He broke the news to me that he had signed me to play a small part in a new musical comedy which was to open at the Winter Garden. Now though this meant a return to Broadway and back to the Winter Garden, I was not to have any connection with the dance arrangements. This was understandable, but I hated the idea of giving up what had now become an obsession with me and I couldn't see how a small part, no matter how important the show might be, could help me to progress. I had given him consent to sign any contract and he had done just this, so I was doomed to honour this new commitment. He accused me (and maybe quite rightly) of becoming big-headed and we parted that night on terms that one could hardly describe as friendly. I received a lecture all the way home from my aunt who claimed I was ungrateful, that Gene knew what he was doing and that I must learn to do as I was told; and that's the way my 22nd birthday party ended.

A few weeks later I reported for rehearsals for the new Winter Garden show and these were held in the room where I first met Jack Mason and joined the chorus of *Innocent Eyes*. I got into the elevator at the Century and there was one other man in the lift who looked at me and said, "Are you the young Englishman who is in the show?" I told him I was and then introduced myself. "My name is Ralph Reader" to which he calmly replied, "I'm in the show too. My name is Al Jolson." How I stood on my feet I'll never know. I was to be in a show with my idol, the great Jolson himself, and then I realised that Gene knew what he was doing. I could write a book solely on my experiences with Al – he always called me "English" – and the help I had from him, the many kind things he did for me, still amaze me and my gratitude to him is tremendous.

Let me give you an example of his kindness.

We opened *Big Boy* in Pittsburgh and toured for ten weeks before coming to Broadway. Four of those weeks we played at the Apollo Theatre in Chicago. Al gave me permission to put on an act at a night club after the evening performance, with six of the girls from the show. It wasn't a top class club, but we gave two performances, one at midnight and the other at 2 a.m. One night, Al came to see us. He sat alone at a table and nobody knew he was there. During the act I used to sing one of his songs *I'm sitting on top of the world* and as I began, to my surprise, he got up from the table, walked to the centre of the floor, put his arm around my shoulder and sang it with me.

Some while ago a very dear friend of mine presented me with a new book on Al which I cherish as one of my most prized possessions. It was written by Michael Freedland and my friend asked that wonderful star of the music hall, Wee Georgie Wood, to write a foreword on a blank page at the opening of the book. This is what Georgie wrote: "February

21st 1973. This is a gift to Ralph Reader, C.B.E. from Douglas Gordon, who has given me the privilege of writing my personal tribute to the man who is now a fellow member of the Grand Order of Water Rats. When he was initiated, it was with pride I told of how my own shows in 1943 in North Africa brought me together with Jack Benny, Dolly Harmer, Gracie Fields, John Steinbeck and Al Jolson. Jolie's first enquiry was for Ralph Reader . . . . this book has one understatement, which is Al Jolson's regard for and opinion of Ralph Reader." Such was the generosity of that superb artiste and great man, Georgie Wood, and no words of mine can thank him enough for that tribute.

I was taken by surprise when I read the book because there were three references to me which were totally unexpected. One particular paragraph affected me deeply. It was about the time during the last war when Al was in England entertaining the American troops. He wasn't very happy at the time but, so the book recalls, "His only happy moment was when he bumped into Ralph Reader and was able briefly to re-live their days at the Winter Garden. "They were great days, English," Al said with a tear in his eye. "Great days". He feared he would never see their like again." It reminded me that this was the last time I saw Al and through all the years I knew him so intimately, whilst others called him "Jolie" or just "Al", I never called him anything but "Mr. Jolson." I've since worked with practically every super-star in show business but not one, in my opinion, ever shone as brightly as the man who will always for me hold the title of "The World's greatest Entertainer."

Big Boy closed at the Winter Garden and went on tour. I left the show and at Gene's command re-started dance producing in small acts, cabarets and rather minor productions far from the big city, and I began th think that I was missing the boat and getting nowhere. Then came the news that *Variety* considered to be of great importance. Gene Buck, who was the right-hand man of Florenze Ziegfield and the

Follies, decided to leave Ziggy and produce his own show. He engaged a star-studied cast and booked the Shubert Theatre. He took with him many of the glamorous show girls who were the pride of the *Follies.* Leon Errol headed the cast and a troupe of Tiller Girls were to be imported from England. The wagers then started as to who would be chosen as the choreographer. Many famous names were then directing the choruses on Broadway – Dave Bennett, Sammy Lee, Seymour Felix and several others. All had great successes behind them – *Rose Marie, Show Boat, Gay Paree, Sunny, The Passing Show,* and *Desert Song* to name just a few, and it became almost a battle as to which of them would be chosen as the dance producer for this new glamour production Gene Buck was to present.

At this time I was with a small show in 'the sticks' where I had produced the ensembles, far away from the lights and the know-alls of Broadway. On a Saturday morning I received a telegram from Gene Macgregor. "Rehearse the girls Saturday morning and see that they give a first-night performance. Love, Gene." What this meant I had no idea, but I did as he told me. I watched the matinée and the girls did well and I remember going backstage to thank them. Then through the pass-door the manager of the theatre said to me, "Who do you think was out front this afternoon? Gene Buck." It was unbelievable that a man of his standing would come out to a small honkey-tonk town to see a touring revue and I almost thought the manager must have been mistaken. I heard afterwards that Mr. Buck had left the theatre before the end of the performance so I assumed he wasn't very impressed with anything he saw. The following Monday morning, another wire came from Gene. "Have signed you to stage the dances for the new Gene Buck Show. Return immediately." I'm not attempting to tell you how I took that news so I must leave it to your imagination, but I took an early train back to New York where Gene was waiting for me and the following day I signed a contract as producer of the dances and ensembles for *Yours Truly*. J.J. Shubert, who was at the opening night, sent for me next day, and I signed a contract as the Shubert dance director for the next five years!

Within three months I had three shows playing in New York which billed me as 'Inventor and Dance Producer' of *Yours Truly* playing at the Shubert Theatre; *Night in Spain* at the 44th Street Theatre and *Cherry Blossoms* at 59th Street. And with all the contracts I wanted right in my pocket I decided that I wanted to come home for a holiday. I felt I had earned it, what's more I had the urge to go back and do a bit of showing off, for the swift success that had come my way had, I confess, given me a big head. There can be no excuse for this because I hadn't done it alone. My aunt had brought me to America, and Gene Macgregor had been my guide, and he alone was responsible for every good thing that had come to me. He gave me a lecture which cut me down to size and some of the home-truths he flung at me went deep. "You've come a long way, Mr. Reader" he said rather sarcastically, "But a couple of flops when you come back can put you straight on the dole, it has happened to better men than you." I cooled down then because I knew the truth of what he had said and, what was more important, he had made me feel ashamed, which didn't do me any harm. Then he helped me sort out my luggage.

This time it didn't mean packing a couple of old suitcases. I possessed a huge American trunk with enough drawers, panels and clothes racks to have accommodated an entire family's wardrobe. Even though I intended staying only a few weeks, I loaded that trunk with all my favourite sweaters, shirts, slacks, shoes – the lot! I intended to create an impression. I sailed on the *Mauretania,* the old four-funnelled pride of the Cunard Line. I was to make twenty-six crossings on this 'Old Lady' and I almost became a member of the crew, making many a trip to the docks for a meal when she berthed in New York and often supplying the purser and his mates with guest tickets for various shows. It was on this first trip home that I became very friendly with Douglas Fairbanks Senior, who was then married to Mary Pickford. We used to walk round the deck together after dinner at night 'to keep fit', and Doug was a genuine 'keep-fit' man, as he certainly had to be in order to perform those acrobatic stunts some of you may remember he used in all his films. One evening, as we were strolling around, some ladies stopped us and asked if he would give them his autograph. He put on his famous smile and duly signed each book like a knight doing his good turn. He bowed to the ladies and thanked them. As we continued our walk I said to Doug, "Don't you ever get tired of being stopped and asked for your autograph?" I'd like to see his reply engraved on every dressing room of every theatre in the world, so that stars and supers, the 'in-betweens' and all beginners could read, mark, learn and inwardly digest his words of wisdom. He said, "Ralph, if you ever get to a position where people recognise you and ask you for your autograph be sure and let them know your appreciation. Sign with a smile, write your name distinctly, and don't hurry. Take your time and enjoy it, because it's going to be terrible when it stops."

It was a splendid voyage all the way home and we were soon steaming into the Channel until there before us was Southampton.

The train journey to Newhaven was very pleasant, for so many things reminded me that I was once more in England. The schoolboys in their school uniforms, caps and shorts, waiting on every station; the hedges and fields; the telegraph poles and the typical railway carriage so different from those I had been riding in for the past seven years. It was a refreshing experience, which I enjoyed to the full. Then we arrived at Newhaven and within minutes I walked into Rose Cottage, which seemed to have shrunk to the size of a telephone booth. It was a great family reunion but I couldn't help being aware of the surprise on their faces as they saw my flash suit, coupled with an American accent that would have made Jimmy Cagney sound like an old Etonian. And so here I was, home again with quite a fair achievement behind me, and at the ripe old age of twenty-four.

5

Home

I had planned to stay around Denton for three or four days and then go to London to see as many of the musical productions playing there as possible. Luckily there were several American friends of mine playing in the West End at the time so I knew I could find plenty of company, even though I didn't know any of the British stars except by name. My first visit when I arrived in town was to the Pavilion where Edythe Baker (with her white piano) was playing in a Cochran revue. Edythe had been with me in the cast of the Jolson Show. My first impression of the London musicals I saw was one of bitter disappointment. They seemed to be slow and dated, and the dance routines I thought were terrible. Even some of the American importations which I had seen on Broadway had lost their flair when presented over here, *Hit the Deck* and *Mercenary Mary* particularly! As for the hotels, well they reminded me of some of the digs I once stayed in during my early tours when I first went 'on the road' in the States. I felt I needed a tonic and there was but one way to be sure of getting just that. So off I went to Ireland and the Dohertys.

I felt re-born the moment I arrived. I stayed for two weeks and every hour was a repetition of the great days I had when I first landed there. The Doherty boys had grown up too but this made no difference – in fact it made it even better. Mrs. McConnell and her family were still living in the same old house and I stayed with them for a few days and then went to stay with Mr. and Mrs. Doherty at the Manse. Show business was hardly mentioned and this in itself was a refreshing change. In fact I think I was plying them with more questions about what had been happening in the village since I left than they were about my adventures on the other side of the Atlantic. Even so, the Doherty boys had reached the age when they were not entirely un-interested in whatever I could tell them about the Broadway chorus girls, and in this direction I was hardly inexperienced! But my stay with them was suddenly cut short. A cable arrived from Gene: "J.J. Shubert wants to meet you in Paris as quickly as possible. Accommodation arranged for you at the Claridge Hotel. Prepare to stay for two weeks." I accepted this as an order (and a pleasant one too as I'd never been to Paris) so within two days from the time I received the cable I found myself in the French capital, where I was to stay for two weeks in one of the finest hotels in the world and it was not costing me a penny. What's more, I was getting paid for it.

The Shuberts had an option on all the novelties in the major Parisian revues and I was to see each of them twice and select anything I thought would be of use to us in our forthcoming Broadway productions. A fortnight of joie-de-vivre in Paris at the height of the season appealed to me and I wasn't disappointed! Luckily I saw very little of J.J. and his entourage and was left to make my own plans and this too suited me. The first revue I saw was at the Folies Bergère and Mistinguett was the star. You will remember I had appeared with her when I was a chorus boy in *Innocent Eyes*

Ralph Reader dancing
with Anna Neagle
in *Limelight*, 1938

S/Ldr Reader and the No. 1 R.A.F. Gang Show
in Normandy, D-Day plus 12

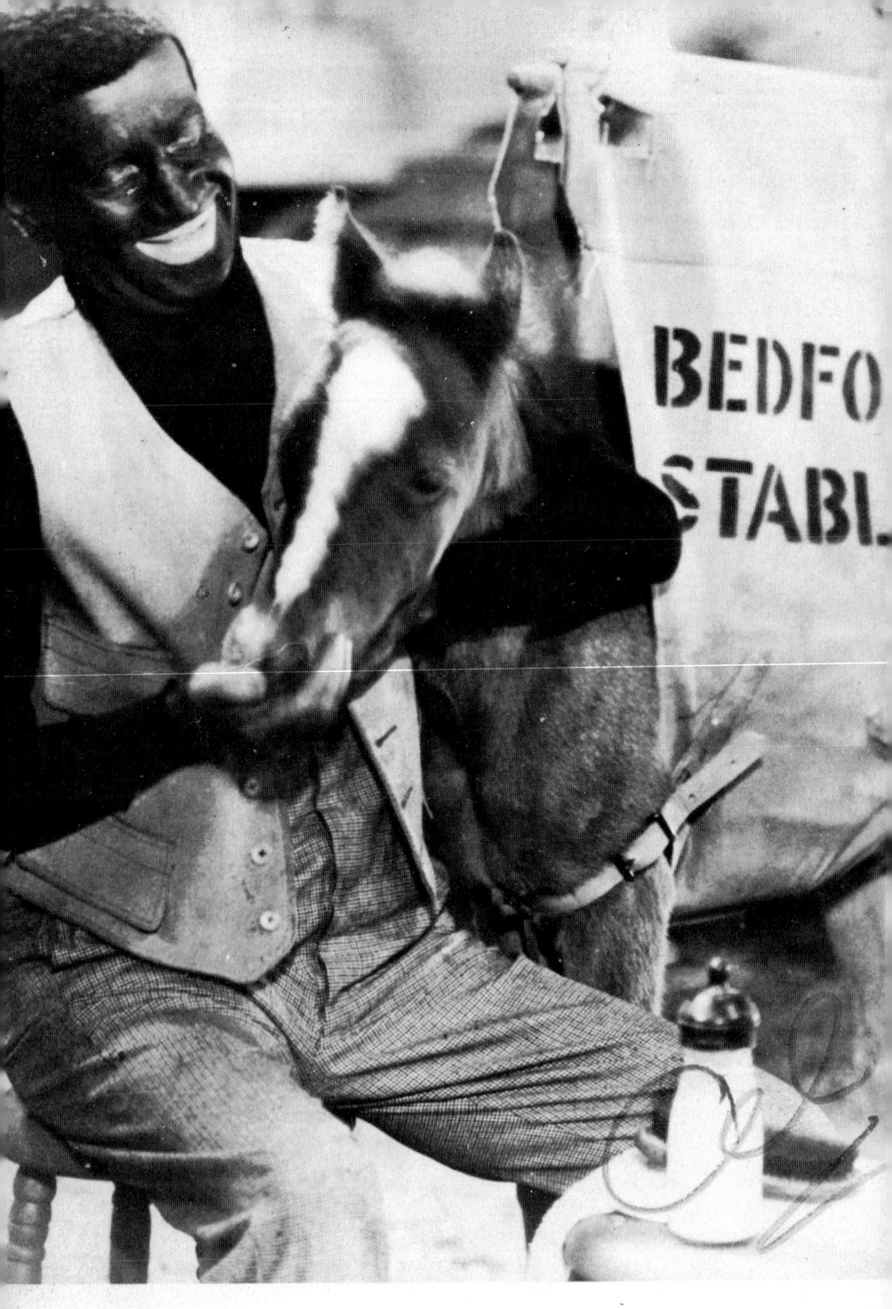

Al Jolson in *Big Boy*, Winter Garden, New York 1926

Ralph Reader with Gina Marlow in the Gang Show film, 1937

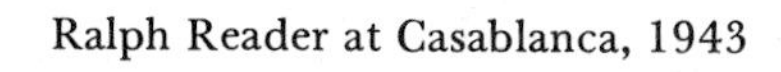

Ralph Reader at Casablanca, 1943

The Service during an annual Royal British Legion Festival of Remembrance

Lord Somers presenting Ralph Reader with the highest award in Scouting, the Silver Wolf, Royal Albert Hall, St. Georges Day 1936

so meeting her again opened many doors for me during my stay there. I was 'living it high' and I made the most of it. "The Dolly Sisters" were starring at the Casino and the Moulin Rouge was another of the shows I had to cover. The splendour of the spectacular scenes in these Paris revues was something I had never imagined and many of them took my breath away. No other city in the world can produce such elaborate productions as Paris and it was a revelation to me to see scene after scene each outdoing the previous one, whilst the beauty of the costumes, and of the staircases rising from the foots to the height of the stage, with dozens of beautiful show girls parading up and down, has to be seen to be believed.

These shows rarely finish before midnight and an evening in Paris doesn't end there. To go on and sample three night clubs in one session was quite the normal thing to do and I fell in with that sort of night-life. Not only did I visit the Lido (where they have the finest of *ANY* night-clubs anywhere) but I also sampled, dropping down the scale somewhat, the bunched-up dozens of lesser clubs around the Pigalle. It wasn't necessary ever to be on my own for I soon discovered one didn't need to speak French to make a date with some fair mademoiselle and it was certainly no handicap to this pilgrim's progress. It was impossible not to find several ideas worth taking back and these I reported to J.J. or one of his entourage. Contracts were signed and I eventually re-staged the novelties in New York. When I think back on some of the world-famous people I lunched with, dined with, and enjoyed the company of, during those electric two weeks in Paris, it reads like a "Who's Who" of Gay Paree. I've already mentioned the Dolly Sisters and Mistinguett and to these ladies can be added celebrities such as Maurice Chevalier, Derval, the creator of the *Folies,* Josephine Baker, Dandy, Yvonne Mendra, Yvonne Printemps and many members of the high society of Paris.

It was a continuous flow of high living. Breakfast in my

room, a bath and a shave and then a stroll along the Champs Elysees, stopping here and there for a coffee and a brandy on the sidewalk outside a cafe, watching the crowds passing by, and noticing how trimly and elegantly the French women dress. Plenty of Americans were passers-by too, and their accent seemed more familiar to me than any Londoners. Several of them, though not having the remotest idea who I was, but recognising the cut of my suit, and knowing immediately that I came from either Brooklyn or Texas, would say, "Swell city, aye?" And I'd make a thumbs up sign. An American makes friends so easily compared with the average reserved Englishman. One elderly man one morning stopped at the table I was sitting at and said, "Mind if I join you?" He had only arrived the night before and had been to see the show at the Lido. I asked him what he thought of it. "Going back again to-night – takes my mind off my wife. I left her behind and it was the cleverest move I ever made." I mentioned what beautiful faces the girls had and he replied, "I hadn't noticed I never got up that far." I asked him how long he was staying and he said with a drawl that could only have come from the South, "We-ell, I figured about a week or ten days, but I ain't in no hurry now."

Sunday, of course, is the big "going out" day in France. Mass in the morning, and from then on it's Fair Day. Every theatre has a matinée and it is also the great sports day, so football claimed two of my Sunday afternoons. Soccer has always been an obsession with me and as they don't play it (or didn't at that time) in America, I was in my element. Every evening of course I spent at the theatre as that was what I was being paid for and I had no objections.

They have very lengthy Intervals at half time and in 1927 the bars in the large vestibules were crowded not only with the patrons but with various ladies whose occupation was easily understood and any gentlemen on his own soon found a "friend" who was delighted to drink with him. It was all part of the scene and a very gay, typical Parisian scene it was

– in fact the ring of the bell announcing the commencement of the Second Act often came much too soon. It wouldn't have met with a Mrs. Whitehouse's approval but there was far less to worry about there than in many dives around the cities of to-day.

Of all the French revues I suppose none are as famous or more spectacular than the *Folies Bergère* and it is nothing short of a miracle how they can stage such gigantic sets on a stage so small. It is only eighteen feet deep and in addition to a rostrum they manage to stage staircases, a swimming pool and equipment which would not be easy to erect at Wembley Stadium. How they can lower down over the heads of the audience in the stalls the famous bird-cage filled with a dozen lovely girls defeats me, but they do. What the cost of such a production amounts to must be astronomical and after the opening of a new Revue, seeing the amount of feathers that are used on the costumes and head-dresses, every ostrich in the world must be bald. I sat through four Paris Revues twice and each time enjoyed them more. Those two weeks in Paris – and at the age when one *SHOULD* enjoy Paris – still bring back some of the memories of my youth in the most satisfying and pleasurable way. And you cannot blame me if I indulge often!

The voyage back to Newhaven was one of the worst trips I have ever had. It's not a long voyage but to me it seemed to last a month. I wasn't actually sick but I was ILL!! The sea was behaving disgustingly and so was the ship and when we docked at Newhaven I felt like falling on my knees and thanking God for deliverance. For days after I could hardly eat a thing and I became so depressed with the dullness of Denton that even trips to Brighton and the Hippodrome almost failed to rouse my spirts. I say "almost" because on one of those trips to the Hippodrome a pal of mine who had appeared in a show with me in New York was on the bill and so were the Houston Sisters. I went out with Renée and Billy for supper and if there is a girl alive today who can swing despondency into a Christmas feeling, that girl is Renée Houston. Today, she is one of our finest actresses. In her act with her sister Billy she was one of the most exciting, beautiful bundles of fun variety has ever discovered. Mistinguett and Marlene Dietrich can boast of their beautiful legs. I'll take Renée! Some of her ad libs during their act would have made even Shakespeare envious (even though she spoke a different language).

I spent another few days in London and then made up my mind to go back to the States. I wanted to start work again and I could find nothing over here that made me feel I wanted to stay out my intended six or seven weeks. So a long week-end back in Ireland, which was a must, then two days back in Denton, and away I went to Southampton to board again the old Mauritania and head back for where I now felt I belonged.

So ended my first visit 'home', but at that time my home seemed to have shifted and as we steamed nearer and nearer to that now familiar skyline I became happier and happier.

6

America 1927-28

A block-busting year!

Gene Macgregor met me when we docked and took me straight to the Winter Garden where I was due to start rehearsals for the staging of the dances for a new edition of *Artistes and Models*. On the way there he told me that Seymour Felix had left the Shuberts to stage a new version of the *Ziegfield Follies* so this promoted me to being their number one dance director and their first choice for all their most important new productions. I told him of the shows I had seen in London and that I longed to go back and show England just what I could do. He wasn't too enthusiastic but he did promise me that he would see what could be done. I gave him a sly glance and his look didn't give me much encouragement. However I was back to a good start and I was rarin' to go. Then he hit me with what I thought was a very unnecessary remark. "You're back to work now, Buddy, this isn't Paris, so cut out the drink, cut out the smoking and CUT OUT THE WOMEN." Now Gene knew very well that (at that time) I never smoked and I never drank, but the last part of his remark was said with a tinge of venom. I understood right away what had happened. He had a pal who was a secretary to J.J. Shubert and had been with us in Paris and it was a certainty that Gene had asked him to keep an eye on me and report back. I could only guess at what this bloke had written to Gene and though it may not have been entirely out of focus it was to say the least grossly exaggerated. I lost my head for a moment and told Gene that if he was employing spies to watch my every move we'd better dissolve our partnership. I reminded him I would be 25 next birthday and I didn't need a chaperone.

Fortunately we arrived at the stage door of the Winter Garden at that moment so the matter dropped. I went on the now familiar stage and met the new chorus and within half an hour we began rehearsals. Gene sat in the stalls all the time and every now and then I would give him the dirtiest look I could muster but not a flicker came back in recognition. At eleven o'clock that night we packed up and I went back to my aunt's where supper was ready for us – Gene of course came too. Then he broke the news to me that he had also signed for me to do another show for Gene Buck and it would have to be fitted in with whatever plans the Shuberts had for me.

To work for Gene Buck again I knew would be a joy but I also knew that the Shuberts were going to keep me busy. They always had several musicals on the road just waiting for one of their New York shows to slow down in business and then they would send me out to polish up the touring show, include some Broadway "names" plus some of their New York girls to supplement the chorus and it would then be brought into New York to replace the show that was beginning to fail. This meant continuously taking sleepers to Boston, Cleveland, Chicago, Buffalo, Cincinatti and all parts west, staying a few days, then back to New York to continue rehearsals with *Artistes and Models* or whatever new presentation they had programmed. To say I was "working" is a bit of a laugh and how I stood up to it I shall never know. But work has always been my number one hobby.

During one of these out-of-town commitments, I became very fond of a little red-head. The girls in these touring shows got very little salary and rarely came to Broadway as the moment the new girls arrived from New York these lesser-lights were switched to another out-of-town Shubert revue. One evening when I took her out to supper she told me that she had to pay 10% of her salary to the dancing school she trained at. This somehow made me sad and I swore that night that as long as I remained in the business I would never accept a percentage from any person I might place in a show. I regret that now! If only I had asked for ONE per cent on some of the boys who have worked with me and have now risen to become household names I would never have needed to work again. And to their credit had I suggested it at the time they would all willingly have agreed. But I didn't, and I have kept that vow to this very day.

It can be nothing but repetition to go into details of the various productions I somehow got through in those following months – shows like *Take the Air, Sunny Days* with the late Jeanette MacDonald, *Countess Maritza,* and a side job assisting Seymour Felix with the *Ziegfield Follies* where I met Fanny Brice, W.C. Fields, Eddie Cantor, Will Rogers and the great Ziegfield himself. I also became a friend of Fred and Adèle Astaire. One of the stars of *Artistes and Models* was the famous Peggy Hopkins Joyce who could always be found on the front page of most of the daily papers. She had married three or four millionaires after graduating from the front line of the *Follies* and though she could never be acclaimed a good actress or singer she was always an attraction and a very fine person she was. On our way to Atlantic City where *Artistes and Models* was due to open, Peggy and I were having a drink in her private compartment on the train. She was showing me some new exotic perfume she had received from Paris when the train gave a lurch and the perfume spilled all over my suit. When we alighted at the station in Atlantic City the whole way to the hotel I was greeted with wolf whistles from porters, travellers and even the taxi driver. When I paid the taxi-man, he smiled quaintly and said, "Thank you dear." Then came the awful moment of going to the reception desk to sign in. Nothing was said but I noticed they selected the oldest bell boy (at least sixty) to carry my bags up to my room and he never even waited for a tip. I guess he decided to take no chances. I never wore that suit again. Can you blame me?

The critics were kinder to me that year than they had ever been before, and I shall always be grateful to such wonderful people as Heywood Brown, Robert Brenchley, Burns Mantle, Alexander Woolcott and Brooks Atkinson. I remember once saying to Bob Brenchley, "How can a fellow like me get his name in the paper." He quickly replied, "Shoot yourself." His knack of shutting someone up can only be described as what the switch does to an electric light bulb.

After the run of *Artistes and Models* I staged the routines for *The Greenwich Village Follies* again at the Winter Garden, but just before this another outstanding event came to pass. I was playing an important part in the Shubert production of *June Days* at the Astor Theatre when it was announced that Al Jolson was bringing back *Big Boy* for eight weeks to play at the 44th Street Theatre. Al was determined to have me return to his show to do one particular number 'Tap the Toe' which had been a big success in the original production. Luckily both shows were the property of the Shuberts so it was arranged that if *June Days* started ten minutes earlier I could rush over to 44th Street and perform in *Big Boy* with Al. So for eight weeks I was playing in two shows on Broadway at the same time.

It was a truly miraculous year, and I was greatly encouraged by some of the compliments the tough New York critics handed out to me. But I was (and am) still learning.

Show business is a profession in which all its members are friends, it is a brotherhood. There is a bond between its members to be found in no other calling. You can leave it, but you will never forget it, and for the rest of your life you will hanker after it. It's a business of hangers-on, yet it is a clan of comradeship. It is the most contradictory profession in the world, for the longer you are in it the less you know. All you ever do is guess and it's just luck which way the guess goes.

Everybody guesses and hopes, whether they are Sir Lew Grade, Bernard Delfont, Paul Raymond or a little comic standing in Charing Cross Road looking for a job. There are *never* any certainties – it's all guess work. Read these words carefully, ye who would enter the portals of the theatrical profession, for then you'll know what you are in for. But you'll have fun and meet some tremendous souls. Never did I realise this more than when I had the honour of becoming a member of the Grand Order of Water Rats. A night I shall always remember.

In America I did nineteen productions and countless vaudeville appearances ranging from the Palace to the smallest and seamiest type of night club which all added to my experience. I owe America something I can never repay, for they took me in, accepted me, trained me and then recognised me, so I felt it was time I started to attack Gene again about the possibility of coming back to London to show what I could do there. The break came in the late summer of 1928 and Gene signed a contract for me to stage the choreography for a new Clayton & Waller show due at the Palace Theatre in Cambridge Circus. It was to be called *Virginia.*

I brought my aunt over with me this time. Gene wanted to come, but after much thought it was decided that it might be wiser for him to stay in America to keep his eye open for future shows when I returned there, especially as my contract with the Shuberts had not yet been completed. So we sailed on the Mauretania and this time I brought with me a flash new car, an open roadster whose like had never been seen in this country (as I was well aware) and though it would look old-fashioned in these days with its cream wire wheels, two spare wheels with patent leather covers on each side of the running board, a mascot of an Indian throwing a spear and two searchlights dominating the sides of the spare wheels, it looked good! Crowds gathered round it everywhere I parked (which was possible in those days). It may have been my way of showing off and I'll forgive anybody who calls me a 'wide boy' because I probably deserved it, but I had hardly taken an hour off except to sleep for the whole of that momentous year and I just felt that now was my hour. My family had moved from Denton to a house in Newhaven and the commotion that car caused when I first drove it into the town is still talked about. I was home again and this time to work and to show London all I had learned from my years in the States.

I took the car over to Magheramorne with me and we did a tour of Ireland which raised a comment from a farmer in Killarney who looked at it for a while and slowly walked away saying, "I don't believe it." I'm sure he didn't either. The only other remark I remember hearing was from an old lady carrying home some peat who said to her companion, "I wonder what it's for?"

The Girl Friend was then playing at the Palace with those great song hits from the pens of Rogers and Hart, *Mountain Greenery, Blue Room* and the title song, *The Girl Friend.* (Years before when Oakie and I were eighteen we knew Larry Hart and Dick Rogers very well and who would have guessed that this great musician, this stupendous composer, Richard Rogers, would one day delight the world with such melodious hits as *South Pacific, The King and I, Oklahoma* and *The Sound of Music?)* I auditioned the chorus girls and boys from *The Girl Friend* to see how many of them

I could use in my forthcoming production of *Virginia.* I took them all. One outstanding girl, Mary Taylor, I chose to be my chief assistant and so she remained for many many years.

So, now on to my first London opening night. Little did I know then how long it would be before I saw Gene Macgregor and Broadway again, and this chapter cannot end without my paying a lasting and sincere tribute to that great friend who did so much for me. God Bless you, Gene.

7

Curtain up in London

The day I started rehearsals for *Virginia* I moved the family up from Newhaven to a house in Norbury where we were to live for the next 29 years. The first rehearsal with the chorus was at the Carlton Theatre while the principals were rehearsing at the Palace. Just before leaving the States, Gene had said to me, "Son, I don't care who the stars are in the show you're going to do and I don't want to read anything about them when you send me the cuttings after the opening. All I want to read about is the dancing of the chorus so use your wits, place your big numbers where you think they will best register and to hell with the principals. Get me?" I got him and I was determined to do just this. My task was made easier (and I say this with respect) by William Mollison, who was to produce the book of the show. He was a brilliant book director and he knew his job, but America had taught me many tricks and I was rather surprised that at all our pre-conferences he agreed with every suggestion I made as to where the main dancing numbers would be placed. The girls and boys were as good as any I ever had on Broadway and we hit it off together from the very start. Herbert Clayton and Jack Waller, together with Joe Tunbridge who was to conduct the orchestra, came along toward the end of my first day's rehearsal and were taken by surprise at the progress we had made. I had been trained to work fast – I knew exactly what formations and steps I needed for the opening chorus and this was completely finished by the time they asked to see what I had done. They were somewhat astounded and made no secret of it. Long before we came to the day when we would join up with the stars everything was set – we were so far ahead of the cast of the show that it took them aback too. We opened in Cardiff for two weeks, then played for a fortnight at Southsea, and finally came our big opening in London. October 25th 1928, saw the curtain rise on the first night of *Virginia.* All the family were there with some other friends and we suddenly discovered that they numbered 13! To me that was a good omen. The first contract Gene ever signed for me was on the 13th and I was living then at 1313 3rd Avenue, so the alleged unlucky number didn't bother me one bit. Just the opposite in fact.

Right from the opening we knew we had a hit. Even that first dance number stopped the show. Another number in the first act the girls and boys did without the aid of music. It was performed entirely by the taps of their feet and this brought the house down. In the second half we had another smash hit with a song called *Roll away Clouds* and we used a shadow effect that created a sensation. The audience cheered and encored until both the singers and the dancers could do no more. Even then the audience were reluctant to let them go. At the final curtain the gallery yelled for the chorus girls and boys and the following morning they took every notice in the national papers. The Daily Mail headlined their notice with "The world's best chorus"; other nationals wrote: "The chorus is the Star"; "The chorus work in *Virginia,* indeed, is about the best that has been seen in the West End"; "The finest chorus I have ever seen." Hannan Swaffer in the Daily Express wrote: "The dances, all of which are very novel and put over by the finest chorus I have seen for a long time, were arranged by Ralph Reader." Finally, the well-known critic, E.A. Baughan, wrote the next morning: "The young men and women of the chorus must be warmly praised and it was only right that the producer who answered the call praised them." After sending the notices to Gene he replied by telegram, "At last you've done as you were told. Now come on home."

But it was not to be. Clayton and Waller had also brought over from New York a successful new musical, *Good News*. They were not satisfied with the leading man and they asked me to join the show. Telephones buzzed, telegrams were sent and even the Shuberts came into the fray until somehow – and I never knew how – it was agreed that I could stay in London to play the lead in *Good News*. So at the Carlton Theatre where the show opened I sang my first song in England, *The best things in life are free. Good News* was before its time and did not have a lengthy run, but I had been in London for several months and I had not been entirely tied to rehearsals and the theatre. I had re-met Hayden Dimmock, the Editor of *The Scout* and he took me out to lunch. He knew that scouting was in my blood and he suggested that by way of relaxation I should look in on a troop based at the Central Y.M.C.A. in Tottenham Court Road. I did and found they were putting on a concert. They asked me for advice which I gladly gave and even attended some of their rehearsals. This meant I got to know several of the boys and in whatever spare time I could find I went around with them. Before I knew it I had joined up again and became a member of the Holborn Rovers. All my enthusiasm for the Scout Movement came back with a vengeance and any free weekend I could find saw me camping with them and then I took on eight young boys who were leaving their troop to become what was known in those days as Rover Squires. I now discovered I had two loves, the theatre and Scouting, both running neck and neck and no one knew which was winning, least of all myself.

After *Good News* came a quick trip back to New York and then home again to stage the dance routines for *Merry Merry* with a cast headed by Peggy O'Neil. On the opening night it was the chorus again who stole the show. Now I promise there will be no more quotes from newspapers praising the dance routines I was producing in those days, but these particular quotes began something which I hadn't the sense to see at the time, so please forgive me if I take from my scrapbook the morning notices after the opening of *Merry Merry*. "Reader is a new force in musical comedy. Principals cannot be expected to hold their own against such dazzling evolutions"; "At the Finale the chorus was at the front and the principals at the back. I have never known a chorus win such cheers"; "Heaven help the Army if they ever engage Ralph Reader to stage the Aldershot Tattoo." To read such tributes begins to make the reader think of taking another size in hats and I was no exception. I was to learn my lesson the hard way.

Show after show followed, mingled with visits to America to fulfill my contracts there, but London was now becoming my home. Then came the 'talkies' and every Hollywood studio was busily signing up every type of artist and producer whether they needed them or not. Their sole idea was to be sure no opposition company got them first. So one night when I arrived home in Norbury there was a cable waiting for me. I opened it and read, "Can sign you immediately dance producer Metro-Goldwyn–Mayer, Salary fifteen hundred dollars a week with three year option, Gene." I still had my hat and coat on and almost in a daze I walked up the stairs to my bedroom and lay on the bed. The fortune I saw staring at me from the ceiling, the dollar bills floating down around me made me dizzy. Fifteen hundred a week and for three years. It was the three years that bothered me. It meant leaving so many things and so many dear friends who had become part of my life. It must have been at least a couple of hours before I came to a decision, then I picked up the telephone and sent a cable. "Sorry Gene, letter following." Next morning I wrote Gene a long letter telling him that I couldn't accept and that I preferred to stay in England.

Whether I did right or wrong in coming to that conclusion can never be known. I might have become a famous Hollywood director—on the other hand I might have been on the scrap heap after those three years. Most things in this world are a gamble and the decision I took that night was surely a big one. Looking back on it now though, I have no regrets. I may not be as rich as I could have been or as poor as I might have been, but the main thing – in fact the most important thing – is, I am HAPPY!

Altogether I have been associated with thirty-four shows in the West End of London. Many were successes and others were flops, but on average I came out on the right side. I eventually took over the entire production of many musicals, doing both the ensembles as well as the book and the whole presentation. My experiences with the great Ivor Novello at Drury Lane remain high in my memories. *Glamorous Nights, Careless Rapture* and *Crest of a Wave* were three productions of Ivor's for which I arranged the ensembles and dances. Nine shows I assisted with at Drury Lane, eleven at the Hippodrome; in fact there are few theatres in the West End that I have at some time or the other not been associated with. A little while back I wrote of "something I hadn't the sense to see" so let me explain what that was because it nearly brought about my downfall.

I had concentrated so much on the dance side of each show I was producing that I resented any of the stars making a hit. Then, one Sunday, a newspaper came out with the headline in very large letters on the Show Business page, "A MENACE TO THE STARS." It then went on to say that principals had no chance if the chorus made the headlines and it could not be good for the show. The public will come to see its favourite star but will never pay money to see just a line up of girls and boys no matter how clever they might be. I confess I was conceited about this article but it had an effect which should have been obvious to me. Contracts became fewer and I suddenly awoke to the fact that I was on the way out. And for about two years I WAS 'out'. I had to take jobs with second-rate touring revues and my hopes of ever getting back to the West End seemed doomed. What's more, my bank account was dwindling and I began to consider begging Gene to get me back to America. The tide turned in an unexpected way. A new show was to be produced at Drury Lane with music by Jerome Kern and book by Oscar Hammerstein, who would also be the producer. The title was *Three Sisters*. There were to be several ballets in the production and two or three ordinary dance ensembles, and it was the latter I was asked to produce. I went along and met Oscar Hammerstein and begged him to allow me to do the ballets as well. Mr. Hammerstein was one of the kindest gentlemen one could ever meet. He understood exactly what I was telling him and my reason for wanting to do the entire musical numbers. I then came out with an idea. I asked him if he would let me prove what I could do with one of the ballets before signing any contract and with no obligation on either side. He smiled and said, "That's fair, Mr. Reader, but you will have to work smartly." The deal was set and I was then played the score of a particularly difficult ballet which I knew my future depended upon. Jerome Kern who was there at the time asked me if I thought I was capable of staging it. I said "Yes" but I was far from sure. However, I realised that I had to take a stand because it would mean either the way back or a finale to my hopes of ever returning to the West End. The few days before rehearsals were to start were terrible ones for me. Confidence is the most important essential in any walk of life and I was beginning to lose mine. To produce a ballet one must be not merely a dance producer but a choregographer and whether I could rise to this I wasn't sure. But the day before we were to start I spent an evening at the Y.M.C.A. with some of my pals from the Holborn Rovers and it turned out to be one of those super parties that completely changed my outlook. My confidence suddenly came back and as I drove home that night ideas began to form in my mind and I went to Drury Lane the next morning with the same feeling I had in my brighter days when I used to drive to the theatre full of eager optimism and assurance. The rehearsal began and after about two hours I saw Mr. Hammerstein sitting in the stalls watching me. We broke for lunch at one o'clock and he came up to me and said, "Let's go upstairs Ralph and sign the contract." I WAS IN!! From then on I never looked back again and though *Three Sisters* was not a success, MY contribution, especially one of the main ballets, *Derby Day,* nearly hit the roof off that great theatre with the applause it received on the Opening Night. Both Jerome Kern and Oscar Hammerstein are now no longer with us, but their wonderful contributions are left to us and will be sung and performed for years to come. I am proud to be able to say that I have worked with them.

Likewise with that other genius of the theatre, the late Sir Charles Cochran. One of my assignments for him stands out above all others. He was arranging a big Charity Cabaret at Grosvenor House and he invited me to stage the musical items. Only Cochran could have assembled such a cast as we had in that Cabaret – in fact it would be easier to say who was NOT in it than to remember who was. The Cabaret was on the night of July 10th, 1935, so allow me to tell you something about it, for few men will ever have the opportunity I had that night to handle so many stars at one time.

One of the highlights of the show was an item, " 'The Glorification of the Body Beautiful', introducing 'Abdaga', the most beautiful girl in the world, discovered by Charles B. Cochran in the Atlas Mountains." Attended by Gertrude

Lawrence, Adele Dixon, Lea Seidl, Heather Thatcher, and a host of other lovely women, the new discovery was escorted (heavily veiled) through the enormous ballroom to the centre stage. It was a marvellous sight.

When the procession reached the centre of the stage the excitement was terrific. It wasn't only the elderly gentlemen who leaned forward to catch the first glimpse of this beautiful woman from the Atlas Mountains. The orchestra halted, came a moment's pause, and then a fanfare. Gertrude Lawrence stepped forward and removed the first veil, then the remaining stars in their turn slowly completed the unveiling until at last the gorgeous 'discovery' stood before the assembly. It was Douglas Byng – in an absolutely stupendous make-up! C.B.'s glorious leg-pull was complete.

The other smash-hit of the evening was a concerted item performed by sixteen 'chorus boys and girls,' and called *Linger Little Lady*. It was a sort of Floradora Sextette, but instead of ordinary chorus 'ladies and gentlemen,' each was a star. Imagine how much it might have cost for a single item, with names such as these in the line-up. Yvonne Arnaud, Edna Best, Fay Compton, Gladys Cooper, Dorothy Dixon, Mary Ellis, Isabel Jeans, Ursula Jeans, Vivien Leigh, Ivy St. Helier, Viola Tree, and Diana Wynyard coupled up with Noel Coward, John Gielgud, Cedric Hardwicke, Nelson Keys, Raymond Massey, Douglas Fairbanks jnr., Owen Nares, Ivor Novello, George Robey, Ronald Squires and my humble self. What a sight for the fans! The following morning I received a telegram from Cocky which read, "Many thanks for all your help, especially for giving me the hit of the evening. I am deeply grateful. Charles B. Cochran." With a cast like that how could I go wrong?

Incidentally, this number gave me my first introduction to Noel. He arrived late for rehearsal but, like the great person he was, immediately came up to me in front of the entire company and apologised. Then he turned and did likewise to the whole crowd. With that he took off his coat and stood ready for instructions. He did more for me in that moment than he ever knew.

The Grand Finale of this Mammoth Cabaret was perhaps as brilliant as anything ever seen or likely to be seen. Assembled on the huge centre stage and lining up even down the gangways between the tables were the entire cast, chorus and all, of *Anything Goes, Glamorous Night, Jill Darling, Gay Deceivers, Love Laughs* and *Stop Press.* Added to this array were still more stars, including Anton Dolin, Jack Buchanan, Robert Helpmann, Laddie Cliff, Tilly Losch, Frederick Ashton, John Mills, Larry Adler and, oh, dozens of others.

At the tables – and there must have been hundreds – sat an audience made up, or so it seemed to me, of every celebrity in the land. All eyes turned to the long illuminated runway which divided the Great Room down the middle and on which the guests were presented to the patrons. And at one table, there sat C.B., pink, cherubic and unflurried, obviously enjoying every act and looking as though he had no connection whatsoever with this gigantic undertaking.

At five o'clock in the morning, the audience long since departed, I sat at a table sipping champagne with Cocky, Delysia, Gertrude Lawrence and Douglas Fairbanks jnr., all of us in a happy glow of satisfaction.

Harold Conway, writing in the Daily Mail, attended the final rehearsal and he wrote in his paper, "I watched yesterday the most remarkable rehearsal in the history of the British stage." He ended his article by saying, "Mr. Reader, I think, was the bravest man in London yesterday." Thanks, Harold, I certainly counted myself the luckiest.

Taking a quick flashback to some of my most enjoyable memories, I remember the fun it was working with Noel Coward and Gertrude Lawrence, staging their dance duets in *To-night at Eight-Thirty* and especially the famous comedy routine they performed in *Red Peppers.* Starring with Frances Day in *The Fleet's Lit up* at the London Hippodrome. My love for Binnie Hale and the run of successes such as *Yes Madam, Please Teacher* and *Big Business.* The films I did with the one and only Dame Anna Neagle, surely one of the most gracious ladies ever. Staging the dance routines for Jessie Matthews in several of her films, and a memory, not dimmed by the years, of sitting one night in a theatre in Detroit with Will Rogers. It was after a performance of one of the shows I did for Gene Buck, one of Will's greatest friends. The audience had gone, and in the darkened theatre we were waiting for Gene who had gone back to talk to a member of the cast. Will, with all the wisdom of that super example of humanity, said, "Gene tells me you are going places, Ralph. As you go on, keep the road decent and tidy. Then you'll be able to look back along the trail and say to yourself, 'Son, it's been terrific'. One final production which still stands out prominently in my memory is *Pilgrim's Progress* which I staged at Covent Garden with Sir Malcolm Sargent conducting and an all-star cast including the dearly beloved Jack Hawkins.

But through all these years it wasn't only the theatre that kept me busy. I had embarked on another venture at a place known as the Royal Albert Hall, and it was here that in 1973 I reached an amazing total of 142 productions. So let me now tell you about these.

8

The Royal Albert Hall

If there is one place in London that has become my home it is the Royal Albert Hall. I know every nook and cranny, every stairway, entrance and exit through all its winding corridors, and the miles I must have walked across that arena and up and down those stairs over the years must add up to hundreds. There have been times when my legs have been so numb that I recalled two lines from the poem *The Battle of Chevy Chase* – 'And when his legs were smitten off, he fought upon his stumps.'

I still feel a certain awe when I realise that I have staged more than 140 presentations in that world famous building.

My first experience at the Royal Albert Hall was in 1934. I had been taken to see *Hiawatha* and I remember how thrilled I was at the spectacle and the glorious singing. Before I went to sleep that night I made up my mind that one day I would do a big show there.

The Boy Scouts Association (as it was called in those days) had long been toying with the idea of showing Scouting in a romantic sort of way to the general public but somehow no one seemed to be able to pinpoint an idea that would do this. Strangely enough, as events turned out, I wasn't too enthusiastic: but I was very keen to stage a show in that enormous hall. One morning, I took a bus to Kensington, walked into the arena, went over to one of the stall seats and sat down. A few visitors were being shown around and suddenly I spotted a small boy standing alone in the arena, with wide open eyes staring at the vast scene around him. He looked like a 'little boy lost' and at that very moment an idea entered my head for a Boy Scout Pageant.

I rushed out of the hall, took a taxi and went home. I didn't even take off my coat but rushed upstairs, took out a piece of paper from the drawer and pushed it into my typewriter. I did not stop writing until the entire first act of *Boy Scout* had been written, and there was only one change in the original manuscript from that moment until the show opened to the public in 1936.

I had to talk over my great idea with a pal and that same afternoon I went to Fred Hurll at Scout Headquarters and told him the story. "You've got it, Ralph," he said, "this is it." I sat down in a chair in his office and then came his next question. "Who can write the music? After all, this isn't Gang Show stuff, it's the Albert Hall." I had an answer for that too. "Fred, I'll do it myself." All he said to that was "Fine." I began writing the score that very evening and had completed two of the songs before I went to bed – *Lift up your Hearts* and *The Night.*

By the week-end every song was written: also the script for the second act. The inspiration was there so I just had to go on with it until it was finished and right out of my system. At last came that final moment when the last note had been written and I fitted the choral numbers and songs into the framework of the script. I read it through and felt satisfied. I believed it was right. All I needed now was permission from Scout Headquarters to go ahead. Yes, all was well, but how many boys would I need? Without hesitation I told them fifteen hundred. How I would manage fifteen hundred people never entered my head.

High on the list was the search for the boy to play the leading role. He had to have every qualification you expect from a film star and yet he had to be a member of the Scout Movement. He must stand up to a supporting cast of many hundreds and yet be able to carry the entire show on his shoulders.

I visited troops all over London but somehow never saw what I was looking for. It began to seem hopeless. One night I had just finished my own Troop Meeting and was sitting in the Headquarters of the 10th Holborn feeling pretty fed up. Most of the boys had gone home and Geoff Birch, my Assistant Scoutmaster, was sitting on a table watching me.

"No luck yet?"

"No." I replied, "none at all." Then from the door of the hall came one of my youngsters. He had left something behind and had come back to get it. He spotted me looking rather dejected so came over to me. "What's the matter, Skip, fed up?" he said. "Just a bit, Len," I told him and looked over to grin at him. The way that kid looked at that precise moment hit me like a ton of bricks. I jumped up from the chair and, turning to Geoff, I said, "Len's the Boy I am looking for!"

I'd combed London from end to end, and here he was in my own troop.

For eight weeks we rehearsed madly and never has a man had such a loyal company to work with. Never a murmur of complaint, never a sign of temperament – all were out to do a job and nothing was going to stand in the way of its being done. On one thing I was adamant. Not one penny did one of those fifteen hundred receive for fares to and from rehearsals, nor for the week's performances at the Albert Hall. No boy or man was to receive anything. To pay for long journeys and food every penny came from their own pockets.

That's the strange thing about Scouts. It's never "What do I get out of it?" but "What can I put *into* it?" They certainly put in plenty. It was a bit tricky handling such a mob but the job never once got out of hand. I called them "Slaves" and they gloried in the word. To clothe such a cast was a mighty problem but again the boys came to the rescue – the boys and, of course, their mothers. Yards of cloth were bought for the Indian scenes, patterns were handed out to each one, and the mothers did the rest.

George Chance took charge of the choir, three hundred strong, and the Whitton boys came along to do their cycling display. The Scout Association had to insure me against getting ill before the show came off, for had anything happened to me it just couldn't have taken place – for the simple reason that all the ideas were in my head, not on paper. Many people said it couldn't be done. Turning a crowd of that size loose in the Albert Hall was asking for trouble; they'd never find their way around the place; they'd get lost; we'd never sell enough tickets to make it pay; we were mad to try it.

But we made each boy realise he stood on his own. There would be no marshals, no guides with tags on them to various entrances. Every member of that vast crowd was to know *exactly* what was expected of him, where he was to go and what his various cues would be. And that is exactly what happened. Each boy was a part of a whole and the whole meant the enthusiasm, the understanding and the complete ability of each individual boy.

To make absolutely sure there would be no missed cues, I chose ten teen-age boys and took them to dinner. I explained that I wanted them to be the Patrol Leaders of each of the dressing rooms. Their job was to be the last out for every entrance, and they were to see every member of that dressing room was on his way to his entrance. Then I said, "Each one of you is to be the Boss of that room and *you* will be responsible for every chap dressing with you. *But* if anyone in that room discovers that you are in charge, I shall ask you to leave the show." I think this is probably the first any of that original cast will know of this. It worked simply because those boys were Scouts.

The dress rehearsal came – and was I scared? Would it all work out? We did a live broadcast which terrified me more than anything I had ever done. The only people who seemed to be taking it all in their stride were those amazing blokes. Young Len Snelling, thirteen years old and starring for the first time in his young life with a gigantic cast supporting him, seemed less concerned than anyone. The Albert Hall seemed to be no larger than their usual Troop Room. On the way home that night, feeling dead beat, I was driving across Clapham Common when the lights of my car suddenly lit up a young Scout walking home. I pulled up and said, "Want a lift, son?" He climbed in and I discovered he was one of the cast. He had lost his last train and was walking home to Balham. He must have been 'out on his feet' but when I asked him how he felt he told me, "Smashing, I'd walk twice as far to be with our mob."

The opening night was one of those experiences that come only once in a lifetime. Packed from floor to ceiling, the show went without a hitch. The stalls, boxes, grand tiers and gallery were a seething mass of people, I went into Len's dressing room just before we started and I have never seen such composure, such confidence, such complete unconcern as he possessed, "Nervous, son?" I asked him. "Not a bit, Skip – we'll paralyse 'em." And they did. From the opening, with the choir in their uniforms and their light blue scarves, singing the songs from the show, success was certain. It was a case of triumph after triumph for everyone concerned. The Indian dance with seven hundred boys in the arena was cheered to the echo, the finale of Act One, with the hundreds of ghosts of the past watching one small boy walk through them on his way to take his Scout Promise was watched by a hushed house, deeply moved by the drama and the sincerity of it all.

At the finale of the show there was an ovation such as

comes only once in a lifetime. But here's the staggering part of it all. When the pageant ended, and everyone was making his way to the exits, not one person, neither Len, nor I, nor Fred Hurll, nor organist Mac, took it as a personal success. It was a team of Boy Scouts who had done a job and on each single one that job had depended; it was a night of team-work, not of individuality, it was the ultimate triumph of Scout training, discipline and reliability. *Boy Scout* had been launched, our critics silenced and now we could await the verdict from the London Press in the morning. They did not disappoint us.

On the final night of the show, long after the lights had gone out and the boys away home, I sat in the artistes' room. I just didn't want to leave; somehow I couldn't. It had been my first effort at a Pageant and my first show at the Albert Hall. I had written the show, composed it and produced it, but that mattered not at all. The real credit was due to those boys from the youngest to the oldest, who had triumphed as only people with a great Ideal before them can triumph. I didn't want to talk, I just wanted to sit and think it all out.

Suddenly a policeman came into the room. He came over to me and said, "Mr. Reader, would you mind coming out and moving your car, please?" I followed him across that darkened arena. I walked up the steps at 'K' entrance and then out to the front door. My car was not where I had left it but at the main entrance of the building. It was decorated from stem to stern with flags and bunting and dozens of Scouts were standing there. I walked toward it and as they cheered I saw something on the bonnet of the car that had not been there before. It was a silver mascot of a Scout and underneath the mascot on a small silver plaque was inscribed: "To Ralph from the Slaves of the Cast. 'Boy Scout' 1936." They pulled the car right round the Albert Hall as they sang one of the songs from the show and I sat there just steering. Believe me, that was just about all I could do.

This particular production of *Boy Scout* was revived

seven times with never an empty seat at any single performance. It is all part of Scout history now, but none who were in that first presentation will ever forget Len Snelling, Jim Figg, Geoff Birch, Fred, Tinny and dear old Mac at the organ.

When the war came I thought it would end my adventures at the Albert Hall but it turned out to be a new beginning. One morning when I was stationed at the R.A.F. Boscombe Down, there came an urgent telephone call for me to report at once to the Air Ministry in London. At Adastral House Air Commodore Strang-Graham told me that the Daily Express were planning a big pageant for the Royal Albert Hall and they had been advised by George Black that I was the man to stage it. My heart leapt at the thought. "You'll get nothing for it, Reader – you must not accept one penny outside of your ordinary Air Force pay, but they will look after you and fix you up whilst you are on this job. We need something like this to help boost morale and Mr. Churchill is very keen about it. Would you like to do it?" What a question! I recall I said almost under my breath, "Blimey." A quick retort came back, "What's that?" "Sorry, sir," I mumbled and he grinned. "Get along to Fleet Street and then report back to me just what it entails."

In Fleet Street I met the 'powers that be' of that great newspaper. Arthur Christiansen, the Editor, and Dick (later Sir Richard) Plummer. Oh, yes, and Tommy Atkins, then Advertising Manager. They asked my views about a show and then brought in "William Hickey," who was to write the script. "William Hickey" in private life was Tom Driberg, the M.P. Within two days we had sorted out ideas, planned a cast of over two thousand and arranged for Sir Laurence Olivier to be in the show.

I told them I should need the assistance of my own particular Gang Show Unit and they agreed. "Where shall I stay while I am in London?" I asked. "We'll fix you up." They did; in a suite at the Savoy. From the wooden camp hut at

Boscombe Down I found myself in a luxurious suite in one of the crack hotels of the world. Good going! It suited me fine.

I met Lord Beaverbrook for about four minutes and all he told me was, "This has got to be a titanic show. I am off to America and shan't be here to see it, but when I return I shall expect to hear it was the finest show ever staged in that Hall." It certainly turned out to be *one* of the finest. Every conceivable branch of the Services was called in, all the Civil Services, and a host of film extras for the crowd scenes. Sir Malcolm Sargent was engaged as conductor. Sargent was not only one of our greatest conductors of classical music – he was a great fan of Sophie Tucker and revelled in Carroll Gibbons. With a wonderful sense of humour, he was the lowest high-brow I've ever met! In my way of talking he was 'a smasher.' In a couple of days he had me prefacing every remark with "With respect. . . . . ." and he in turn was using my phrases of "terrific" and "smashing."

The Pageant told the story of England. We tried all sorts of tricks, once nearly blowing a hole in the Albert Hall when we tried a too-realistic bomb explosion effect in an air raid. They made me cut it out. We had raiding Commandos coming through a fifty-feet cloud of real steam. To get this steam going we used the blowers of the organ and it worked well. (Of course you couldn't play the organ at the same time!) We staged an Air Raid with messengers on motor-bikes madly careering round the arena dodging the various Fire Brigades and Rescue Parties.

Somehow I don't think the Bishop of Kensington will forget his first rehearsal with us. He was to take a short service. The several hundred film extras in the show were playing every part imaginable. When the Bishop arrived in his robes he asked one of these characters the way to the stage. I dread to think what he thought when the reply came back. "For gawd's sake, mate, you've been rehearsing for blank-blank-days, surely you blankety well know the so-and-so entrance to the stage by now." (The extra naturally did *not* say "Blankety-blank.")

Perhaps the biggest thrill of *Battle for Freedom* was a pat on the back from the Prime Minister. Mr. Churchill did not stay for the entire show – he had to be back at No.10 – but he saw me for one moment and said, "Good, *very* good." That was all I wanted.

We eventually took the Pageant lock, stock and barrel to the King's Hall, Manchester. It was while we were here that news came through of my award of the M.B.E. As soon as it was announced, one of my blokes came to me, "Congratulations, Chief, do we have to call you Dame now?"

As I have already mentioned, *Battle for Freedom* was sponsored by the Daily Express and again quoting from letters sent me, especially one from that great man of Fleet Street, Arthur Christianson, it reads, "You promised me at the outset this was to be the show of your life. . . . . I realise the tremendous effort you made to fulfil that promise. The best thing in the show I am told was yours. When I say that I am thinking of the electric surprise throughout the audience when the Altmark sailor bawled out his message from the roof.I am personally envious of your high skill and splendid inspiration." No human being could be other than proud to get such a letter.

The night after we had given this show, with everything at our command and a gigantic cast of thousands around us, I was playing with my ten airmen on a tiny Station in the South of England. The only entrance to the stage was up a ladder and through a truck, and the dressing rooms were in a tent over a hundred yards away.

Of all my Royal Albert Hall productions, I rate as Number One, the Annual Remembrance Festival for the British Legion. There is a polish about everything connected with this enterprise which is a joy to all who take part. Dignity is the key-note; and with its precise timing this Festival is a never-to-be-forgotten occasion. Now, millions throughout the country can see it on television. But only in the Hall can one really appreciate the magnificence of the pageantry, the colour of the uniforms and the genuine warmth of the Royal Family's presence. I know no other moment so charged with feeling as when, through the distant sounding of Reveille, the Poppies, like scarlet snowflakes, flutter down from the dome of the Hall to cover the servicemen and women standing in the arena. It is an emotional experience and every one of us who has some small hand in this great Festival is to be envied.

The Royal Naval Pageant was another very ambitious production, again with a cast numbering over 2,000. I am often asked how I manage to handle such crowds. To me there is no such word as "crowds" – I look upon them as PEOPLE and when I am directing them I try to make them feel I am speaking to each one individually and, praise be, they realise this. In this Pageant, *Heart of Oak,* we had a wonderful cast of principals. Sir Vivian Dunn directed the Symphony Orchestra of the Royal Marines. Wally Patch, Beatrix Lehmann, Frank Phillips, Nicholas Parsons, Martita Hunt, Peter Croft, Sir Alect Guinness (who was then a Lieutenant in the R.N.V.R.) and many others. Next morning came a telegram from the Chief of the Naval Staff addressed to me which read, "This is just to congratulate you on your magnificent work. You have done a fine job for the Navy and we are all very grateful. I have heard nothing but praise from all sides."

To name all the varied presentations I staged at the Albert Hall would be impossible, but obviously certain ones stand out above others. I'm a sentimental man and I make no bones about it and I remember well on one occasion bringing together those two great stars of other years, George Robey and Violet Lorraine, and having them sing their immortal duet from the First World War, *If you were the only girl in the world.* I forget how many encores they were forced to take. Then there was the night I wrote and produced a performance for the Old Contemptibles. No greater nostalgic evening could ever be. I mentioned sentiment a moment ago and the last pageant I produced for the Royal Air Force before I was demobbed stands out head and shoulders above many of the others. It was to be a colossal spectacle telling the whole story of the R.A.F. from its birth as the Royal Flying Corps and right up to the present day. The cast was to number 2,300, all of whom were in the Royal Air Force. To rehearse this the Air Ministry re-opened an R.A.F. Station at Chipping Ongar and there the cast assembled. Some by lorries, cars and planes. They came in from Stations all over the country. A Wing Commander was put in charge of the Station but otherwise it was all mine. For two weeks we rehearsed all hours of the day and night and I had a young sergeant standing by with me all the time looking after my scripts. His name was Richard Attenborough! We all became a big family.

Outside the Headquarters in white chalk on the foreground were the letters "R.A.F." Some wit one night changed this and next morning we read, "READER'S AIR FORCE." Finally, the day came when everyone left to hold the final rehearsals at the Albert Hall. After they had all gone I drove around the empty camp knowing full well that this was likely to be my very last contribution to the great Service I had loved. The empty huts, the bare hangars where we rehearsed, now so quiet and still, with no sound anywhere, told me this was the beginning of the end to an era of my life. Sir Winston Churchill once said that if you lose sentiment you become an animal and though happy I felt a loneliness around me that is impossible to explain. I got out of the car and kicked away the letters of chalk outside the H.Q. and then got in the car and drove away.

"Per Ardua Ad Astra" (the script had been written by Alan Melville) turned out to be everything we had dreamed about, and the next morning came a letter from Marshal of the Royal Air Force, The Viscount Trenchard. "I must write you a short note as President of the Royal Air Force Association to thank you on their behalf and on behalf of many other friends of mine for what you did to make the Royal Air Force Pageant such a brilliant success. It showed genius to bring out so clearly the spirit right from its earliest days. May I add my deep personal thanks to you." As if this weren't enough, the very next day I received another letter from him which read, "Dear Reader, I must just send you another note after last night. I fear the letter I sent you yesterday was inadequate. You have done magnificently." Darlington in the Daily Telegraph wrote, "It was a spectacular triumph." If using these quotes may appear rather like an attack of ego, I apologise, but they are in my scrap book and I am not ashamed to tell you that now and again when I'm feeling a bit fed up I read them and recover. Lord Trenchard will for all time be regarded as the "Father of the R.A.F."

Producing these enormous pageants never seemed like work to me because I got such enjoyment out of them. There was always plenty of humour which would suddenly appear at just the right moment. I remember a W.A.A.F. Officer coming to me during a break at one of the Festivals of Remembrance. "Ralph" she said, "How many shows have you done at the Albert Hall?" I told her at that time it was 97. She said, "97!! What, annually?" From then on every time anyone asked me how many productions I had staged there I would say "102" and then quickly add, "but not annually." I bit the dust one morning though when a young matelot put his hand on my shoulder and asked the same old question, as to how many shows I had done there. Quickly I told him 110 but not annually. He looked straight at me and then said, "You mean you missed a couple of years?" You can't win!

A feature of the Coronation Ball for our present Queen was the *Masque* which I staged with a cast of star names that would cover several pages from *Who's Who in the Theatre*. Then there was the annual radio transmission *To you America* (on each Independence Day) in which Sir Winston

Churchill played an important part. Mr. Churchill (as he was then) had given me a cigar on at least four occasions and he once said to me, "It's about time you gave *me* one." The opportunity came when I was connected with the Alamein Reunion. He was sitting in a box with General Eisenhower, General Montgomery, Mrs. Churchill and Mrs. Eisenhower. I walked over and handed him a cigar, cameras flashed, and next morning the front page of several newspapers carried the picture. It is one of my prized possessions and this same photograph is included in a book, *The wit of Churchill.*

Another great night for me is when I produce, again annually, the Burma Reunion. There is something about this event which stands out in some incredible way. Perhaps it is because they still remember they were, for a long while, 'The Forgotten Army.' General Sir William Slim ('Uncle Bill') is no longer with us, but the Earl Mountbaten holds us all together and makes this occasion always a night to remember. Strangely enough, even with the passing of the years, this night seems to get mightier every time and next to the falling of the poppies in the British Legion Festival nothing can approach the warmth, in fact the magic, of the moment when the one and only Vera Lynn walks on to the stage and sings to us. Vera *belongs* to us and every man in that vast audience would be happy to listen to her for hours on end. Who else in the whole of the Theatrical Profession can sing, "Yours," "The White Cliffs of Dover" and perhaps above all, "We'll meet again" as this unsurpassed lady can and bring together the hearts of all who so rightly worship her. There is only one Vera Lynn and we shall never see her equal. She belongs to every Service Man in the last war and to every civilian who, though they may have been staying in Britain, were still in the front line, and these words are but a small tribute to one who has done so much. Take it from me, the Burma Reunion is an outstanding occasion. How lucky I am to be associated with it.

Throughout many of these spectacular presentations

there was always by my side a man who contributed more than any other toward their successes. This man is W.A.Sutton, known in those days to us all as Bill. Bill and I have been together since he was about fourteen and today he is a very important person in his own right. Not only the head of one of the biggest P.R. Managements, but also as a Producer. He has made a terrific success of his life and I proudly pay tribute to his ever present advice and contribution to many of the things I have been able to do. Without him it may well have been impossible. May everything good come to him throughout his entire life. In the latter years his place has been taken by my son, Bob, but you will be told more about Bob in another chapter.

Looking back on my productions at the Royal Albert Hall, there has only been one that I remember with a shudder. It was called, *Contrasts* and was sponsored by the Outward Bound Trust and somehow or other they enticed the Scout Association to join in with the idea of splitting the profits. I was asked to produce and in a moment I shall never cease to regret I agreed. Unknown to me at the time, they had already contracted a number of Acts and when they showed me the list of performers I came to as near fainting as I have ever done. They were mixing (hence the title) various very modern Pop Groups and singers with a young Classical Pianist and other high-class vocalists specialising in serious music. In addition, they had engaged a very well known comedian whose jokes go far beyond what would be suitable for the higher-minded type of audience who would also tremble at some of the full-blasted instrumentalists and singers of the Pop Groups. Likewise the Pop followers would never stand for the more serious side of the entertainment and I made my views very clear at the first meeting that the organisers would be heading for trouble. I should have bowed out there and then – my instinct told me such two different audiences would resent each intrusion to what *they* wanted and there was bound to be a certain element who wouldn't be afraid of airing their feelings. And they weren't! As the night wore on, all I feared came to pass, and ultimately it became so bad that for the first and only time in my life I walked out, went to the nearest pub and knocked back a stiff drink. How it ended I never knew but as the Producer I was entitled to the blame and I got it. Not only by letters but also by phone calls. It was useless for me to try to explain that I had not engaged one single act –that it had all been done before I took charge – I caught it good and proper. I was even blamed for some of the 'jokes' that were told and as I had no idea what jokes were going to be told I felt a few of my critics were going a bit too far. However, I learned my lesson for never again would I undertake to handle *any* presentation unless I knew beforehand who was to be in the cast and what their performance would consist of. Not for the greatest Charity on earth will I again go blind-folded into such a night and one I still regret with all my heart.

However, time makes people forget and I more than made up for it soon after with "A night with the Stars" and this is really what it was. Just imagine the excitement of those electric three hours when on the Bill I presented such stars as: Eamon Andrews, Dame Margot Fonteyn, Kenneth McKellar, Leslie Crowther, Russ Conway, Michael Bentine, Frankie Vaughan, Dame Anna Neagle, Jack Parnell and his Television Orchestra, Norman Vaughan, Hughie Green and Mike Yarwood. Nor must I forget an act which was *not* professional and yet made just about the biggest hit of the night – the 13th Coventry Scout Band. They were such a success that Jack Parnell's entire orchestra stood up and applauded them. The ovation they received was sensational.

Like all things in one's life, it is the successes one remembers most and I have had my share and far more than I may have deserved, so to all the thousands who have shared with me those great nights in that memorable Hall may I say a "Thank you" to every one of them because it was *they* who finally brought to life any and every single idea I tried to create.

And remembering that, it is natural I suppose that I often feel a very humble man.

9

The Gang Show

Well, it had to come didn't it? Like Morecambe and Wise. Marks and Spencer, Colman and mustard, the Gang Show and I go together. It forms an integral part of my life. A great number of people still think this is the only thing I have ever done. It isn't (as you will have read) but many think of me only as "Mr. Gang Show" – full stop!

I remember, when I was the subject of "This is your Life," the hundreds of letters that came to me expressing amazement that I had been connected with "the real stage" and knew and directed "real actors." Even today, I have to admit that this fantasy still exists and I've long since given up trying to stop it. Like the Niagara Falls, it goes on and on as if I have no other interest in my life whatsoever. Ye gods, I'd have been on the bread-line for years if this had been the case. So let's get down to the beginning and see how it changed my entire life.

One momentous morning, I went to the Scout Headquarters in Buckingham Palace Road to have lunch. I was rehearsing a show for the Palace Theatre at the time and whilst waiting for the lift I was joined by the then County Commissioner for London, Admiral Philpotts, who was also on his way to the restaurant. He had seen some of the shows I had helped with at St. George's Hall in the Central Y.M.C.A. in Tottenham Court Road for the Holborn Rovers and he asked me if I would consider putting on a bigger type of show to raise funds for a swimming pool at one of London's camp sites near Downe, Kent. Without doing much thinking, I said, "Yes, as long as it's not to be an old-fashioned trek-cart display," which is what most Scout concerts consisted of in those days. The year was 1932. The only other stipulation I made was that my name was not to be associated with the production. At that time I had three major productions running in London and I didn't want to get mixed up with a Scout show that could go either way, good or bad. I left him at the restaurant and ate at a table with two of my closest friends in Scouting – Fred Hurll and "Tinny" Fellows. I told them of the idea and they fell for it to such an extent that their enthusiasm clinched the whole matter for me. By the time the three of us had finished eating we had laid out a programme which was never changed from that moment to the opening night of the show.

We needed a cast of about a hundred and fifty boys. Some of these we knew we could recruit from Holborn and we felt certain a lot of our pals in Harrow would come in with us. In addition, we had connections with numerous Scouters in Hornsey and we came to the conclusion we could get all the numbers we wanted from these three Districts. This is exactly what happened, and we held our first rehearsal on May 25th, 1932 – my 29th birthday! We already had various items we could salvage from the old Holborn shows and I felt I was capable of writing sufficient extra material to make up a programme. It was planned to run the show for three nights.

Then came the question of a title. The first suggestion

seemed a good one. As it was for Downe Camp, some bright spark suggested "Downe and Out," whilst another thought "Up Downe." These were both worthy ideas, and found favour amongst the gathering crowd who would be in the show. Within a matter of weeks we had booked the Scala Theatre and started rehearsals. Enthusiasm was high and we all had the feeling that we were on to a good thing. Eventually, it was time for posters to be printed but I still wasn't sure about those titles. Then, one night, we hit the jack-pot. We had stopped for a cup of coffee, and having called the boys back, I said to a youngster, "Is everybody, here, son?" Quick as a flash he replied, "Aye, aye sir, the gang's all here." It hit me like a bullet. "THE GANG'S ALL HERE." *That* would be the title of the show! So the posters were produced and then came the task of selling tickets. On the second night of the show we had arranged for members of the Royal Family to be present, so we decided we could charge extra on that occasion. Now the Scala holds (or did hold) only just under a thousand seats, but we suddenly awoke to the fact that nobody wanted to buy tickets.

I'd go to friends and say, "Would you like to see a good show?" and they'd say, "Sure, but what is it?" When I replied "It's a Scout show," that did it! They all suddenly discovered they had a date for that night and wouldn't be able to attend. It became obvious to us all that we were not going to have a Box Office success and our spirits sank. However, there was the middle night when Royalty would be present, so, with the extra charge, we might be able to break even.

We opened on October 30th, 1932, to half a house and with the Chief Scout and his wife sitting in a box. When I ventured out front before curtain time I realised that there would be more people on the stage than there would be in the audience. Up went the curtain to this very thin house, and even then many of those present had been invited as guests and therefore hadn't paid for their tickets. But the show went well, VERY well in fact, and the enthusiasm at the end was startling. The next night we were to have the Duke and Duchess of Kent to play to, and that should have meant a full house. It didn't! What's more they couldn't even turn up. There were serious labour troubles at the time and it was thought inadvisable for them to leave the Palace. However, we had three quarters of a house, although there was natural disappointment amongst the audience that they were not going to be present with Royalty. Yet the applause for the show was even greater than it was on the previous night, and when the curtain fell there were cheers. After this performance, the Chief Scout said to me, "Reader, this is good propaganda for the Movement. It is a means of reaching people outside Scouting. Will you do another show next year?" Frankly, I thought he was utterly wrong, but as the request came from the Chief I said, "Yes, I will." The third night we nearly filled the theatre and this brought new heart to us all. At the close of that final performance the audience stood up and yelled for more, and we must have sung every song in the show all over again. So ended the first Scout Gang Show.

The posters announced the show as being written and produced by "A Holborn Rover" so no one in the profession had the slightest idea of my connection with this event – in any case, hardly anyone even knew the show had been put on. Well, the second year we called it "The Gang comes Back," and to our surprise we did well. No full houses mark you, but ten times better than in the previous year, and this time we ran for five nights!

The spirit of the Gang was something only Scouting could produce and we booked the theatre for the following year to run for a week and a half. This was 1934 and it was then that I wrote for the finale of the first act a song called, *We're riding along on the crest of a wave*. Who could have realised just how high we were riding? Certainly not I. One of the stalwarts of the cast was Jack Beet, a sacred name to every boy who had ever appeared in a Gang Show. He was Rover Leader of the 4th Harrow and a keen and fabulous Scouter and a splendid performer. The 1935 show was booked for two weeks and we were sold out long before it was due to open. We conceded that B.-P. had been right in his judgement and the Gang *did* mean something to Scouting. Up to now the Gang Show had played only in London but Scouting visitors from the provinces had come down to see what we were doing and decided to stage a show in their own cities. Newcastle and Glasgow were among the first and both shows turned out to be gigantic successes. By 1936 there was no holding the demands for seats and the Press became interested. They came along, saw the show, and at once caught on to the fact that a professional *must* be behind it. They wanted to know who this professional was and I was equally determined they shouldn't. They gave rave notices to the show. The Daily Mail said, "The best revue in the West End." The Times wrote, "This is quite magnificent. . .it is genuinely moving and impressive." The Morning Post wrote, "Speed and brilliance in new Scouts Revue. . .flawless efficiency. . .not a single professional show in the West End which could not learn something from it." The Telegraph came up with, "This is one of the best shows of its kind I have ever seen. There is an abundance of wit, caricature, satire and plain knock-about comedy. It is impossible to enumerate all the good numbers." We were away!

It's all history now; the show spread not only to the other major cities in this country but also overseas, and Canada, New Zealand and Australia started producing Gang Shows. They used all the original material from the London show and no charge was ever made for a single sketch or item which I had written as I turned everything over to the Scout Association and such a thing as royalties just did not exist – and never have throughout the years.

One is often tempted to forget the smaller Gang Shows – the Group Shows – which seldom get mentioned in the same way as those playing in larger cities. Yet they belong to us – a little village show in Malaya just as much as a larger theatre version. We all belong to the one family of Red Scarf gangsters who (and let us never forget this) have been joined together solely because of our belonging to what must always have our greatest loyalty – the Scout Movement.

Now, there is one name which *has* to be remembered when any history of our shows appears in print. It is the name of a man who gave his entire life to the world of Gang Shows. He was known to countless thousands who had never met him but knew about him and received from him letters, scripts, music and a personal touch that is a legend amongst us all. That man was Tommy Thompson. A volume could be written about Tommy. I know of no man who had to endure such hardships as Tommy – his state of health was enough to break any lesser man. He was almost completely deaf and his sight made visibility impossible beyond just a few yards. Yet no mention of these afflictions ever passed his lips, and he knew more people throughout the world of Gang Shows than even I did. I recall that on one occasion when I visited South Africa, a young thirteen-year old Scout came up to me in Durban and asked, "How's Tommy?" I knew he had never met him nor would he ever see him so I enquired how he knew about Tommy. His reply was typical. "Oh, he writes Skip such fine letters and they are always read out to us at Troop meetings. He's a great fellow isn't he?" Tommy Thompson had the love of everyone who ever had anything to do with a Gang Show. He has "gone home" now and I miss him in a way I can barely understand. There will never be a more loyal person than Tommy, nor one with more courage, and I hope these few words will stand for all time as a tribute to a really great Scouter.

Throughout those early years the demand for seats grew and grew until for weeks prior to the show there was not a single ticket to be had. Then the Press stepped in and insisted on getting information. They demanded to know who the person behind it all was, and I was still determined not to allow my name to appear. The Scout Association decided there was only one thing to do. They would give a lunch to the Fleet Street men, explain who *was* behind the show and tell them *why* I wanted to keep it separate from my West End commitments.

The lunch was held at the Victoria Hotel and many of the press lads having drinks before the lunch asked me what *I* was doing there. I kidded them and dodged the question. However, after the lunch ended the chairman of the Gang committee put the case forward for me and explained in detail why I did not want my Scouting life to be involved with my professional career. Dear old Hannan Swaffer was there and he and the editor of the Morning Post, S.R. Littlewood, said right out that they intended to tell in their newspapers the following morning just who the producer and writer of the show actually was. Next morning, every newspaper carried the story and 'A Holborn Rover" vanished from the scene. From then on, all billing for the Gang Show was changed to "Written and Produced by Ralph Reader."

I was doing the choregoraphy for Ivor Novello in all his Drury Lane shows at the time – *Glamorous Night, Careless Rapture* and others, and he and his company came to our dress rehearsals. We were getting more and more publicity and one evening in his dressing room at Drury Lane, Ivor had a serious talk with me. The Gang Shows had now begun to spread all over the world and Ivor was a keen observer. He said to me, "Ralph, get rid of this Scout show. If you don't it will swamp you and beat you. You will become known only as the Gang Show man and this is certain to hurt you professionally." How wise were those words. Looking back on the years I have to admit that, had I known what the future was to bring me, I honestly believe I would have done just what Ivor advised. *But* – with all the great mates I had made, the fun and the comradeship – it was all too difficult. I just could not do it, so I skipped Ivor's advice and stayed with the

Gang.

We went from strength to strength and before I realised it I became known as "Mr. Gang Show." Never was this brought home to me more convincingly than one evening at Covent Garden where I had produced *Pilgrim's Progress.* I was standing at the stage door waiting for Malcolm Sargent, who was taking me out to supper. Two dear old cockney women were passing and stood looking at the bill outside the theatre and one read it out aloud. "Look, *Pilgrim's Progress* produced by Ralph Reader. Nobody would have heard of him if it hadn't been for the Boy Scouts." That took quite a bit of swallowing.

Then came the film. I had been working with Herbert Wilcox for some time and had arranged the dances for Anna Neagle in a number of her films and also appeared in them. Herbert decided he would like to film "The Gang Show" and film it he did. And what a wonderful experience it turned out to be for the Gang. The filming took place at Pinewood Studios, where a number of other films were being made at the same time, and many of the stars took a delight in coming to see the boys at work. One story I must tell you, although I cannot vouch for it being completely true. One morning the fabulous Marlene Dietrich came in to watch us and when it was time to break, she said she would like to take about four of the boys to lunch in the studio restaurant. Asked if she had any preference for the ages of the boys, she is alleged to have replied in that dreamy, husky, romantic voice, "Vell, for lunch, about thirteen or fourteen, but for supper, twenty-one!"

We had our fair share of funny incidents at the Scala Theatre too. I remember one night when the opening chorus had ten policemen on stage. I happened to be at the stage door where a genuine policeman was standing. Unthinkingly I grabbed him and said, "Mate, you'll miss the opening." He came down stage with me and just as I was pushing him on he grabbed me and said, "Hold it chum, I'm no actor, I'm on the level."

In 1937, the film was released with myself as the star and it opened at the Lyceum Theatre. It was a brilliant night and the Evening News next day came out with the headline, "London has a new Film Star."

Big Business was running at the Hippodrome at the time and I had devised the entire production as I had with the previous shows there, *Yes Madam* and *Please Teacher.* I was then due to return to Drury Lane for their next show, but already theatre managers were talking about my major interest (or so they thought) in Gang Shows! Nothing could have been further from the truth, but there it was and it began to stick. To bring them even more into the public eye, the Gang were selected as the first amateurs to appear in the Royal Command Performance at the London Palladium, lining up with such stars as Gracie Fields, Florence Desmond, Cicely Courtneidge, Will Fyffe, George Formby, Max Miller and a host of others. One little incident comes to mind which I do not think any of us will ever forget. As the King and Queen were leaving the box, Her Majesty waved to the audience and then to the cast on the stage. As she looked down on the boys in the Red Scarves, she gave them a special wave. It was a *very* special wave and the audience rose to it and spontaneously broke into even louder cheers. The B.B.C. narrator spotted it and said over the air, "Ralph Reader must be a very proud man tonight." He was indeed proud, and so were his boys. The papers came out next morning with the ratings that gave the number one hit as Max Miller and number two, the Gang Show. For that, George Black booked us for a week at the Palladium. You see, you just couldn't stop this avalanche.

One good break, however, did come my way. George Black engaged me to play opposite Frances Day in a big musical, *The Fleet's Lit Up* at the London Hippodrome and I was also to stage the dances. *This,* I thought, would be my salvation. We played for over a year, which brought us into

1939. WAR! At last, at long last, I began to see that the Gang Show would have to fold up and I could escape. I was already tied up with the Royal Air Force as I've explained elsewhere, so I thought to myself, "When the war is over – no more Gang Shows." I was convinced that my only hope for the future was to give all my time to the professional theatre. Ye Gods, what a hope! The week before war was declared I was playing in a variety act at the Coventry Hippodrome and the following week we were due to play at the Kingston Empire. It was not to be. Sunday came, we were at war, and all theatres were closed. That same week, instead of appearing at the Kingston Empire, I was wearing the uniform of a Pilot Officer in the Royal Air Force.

We had a Gang Show ready for that October and the memories of its final rehearsal are still fresh in my mind. We met as usual in the Drill Hall at Chenies Street, and I had to tell the boys there could be no show owing to the war. It was a truly pathetic farewell. The tenseness of their faces, the knowledge that so many of the lads before me would soon be wearing a different kind of uniform and that some of them might never again be with us to join in our songs, made it a moving moment. After seven glorious years together, we knew this meant the parting of the ways. We said our goodbyes, and all sang *These are the times we shall dream about.*

The song took on a new and poignant meaning. The saddest breaking-up I shall ever see then took place: the boys, without a smile, just quietly shook hands, said "so-long," and wandered off to their homes. Over thirty of those boys did not come back, and of all the many pictures of the London Gang Show which have been taken over the years, the one I treasure most is of the final scene in the Gang Show film, for no less than ten in the front line alone are amongst those who never returned.

War, with its menace to liberty, was with us again, and until it was over – no more Gang Shows. To those lads who

H.M. The Queen backstage
at the 1957 Gang Show
with Ralph Reader and
Sir Charles McLean, the Chief Scout

Battle for Freedom,
Albert Hall, 1942.
Speaker Sir Lawrence Olivier

Per Ardua Ad Astra, the Albert Hall, 1946, which Ralph Reader produced with a cast of over 2,000 airmen. (Note the airman who fainted in the centre row being held up by his colleagues)

Arrival at O'Hare airfield, Chicago, 1958, for the first American Gang Show

Dick Emery tells
Eamonn Andrews and Ralph Reader
his memories of the R.A.F. Gang Shows
during the T.V. show
This is your Life – Ralph Reader

El Alamein Reunion, 1951.
Ralph Reader presents a cigar
to Winston Churchill
while Field Marshall Montgomery
and General Eisenhower look on

Christmas morning, 1973.
Ralph with his two grandsons,
William and Stephen

had been with us, who formed the "Gang Show" and who started the great institution that was eventually to become even more famous, let us pay our thanks and say to each and every one of them, "God Bless."

How was I to know that throughout the coming war years Gang Shows would be recreated and destined to cheer the troops on every battle front of the world? Yes, and even in German prison camps.

Farewell then to peace and to Part One of the Gang Show story. The second part was to bring forth some of the brightest stars in show business today and to blaze a trail across India, Burma, the Middle East, Normandy, and finally beyond the Rhine.

10

The Royal Air Force and World War Two: Part 1

Let me start by explaining how I first became involved with what is called the Junior Service. I appreciate that the Royal Navy is the Senior Service but forgive me for saying that to *me* the Royal Air Force will always be the Superior Service, I suppose because I wore its uniform, and how that came about is quite a story of one man's way-ahead thinking.

On the committee of the Gang Show was Major Archie Boyle, an ex-Army man and one of the finest gentlemen I have ever met. He was closely connected with Scouting and a District Commissioner for Lambeth North. He and I were great friends and we spent a lot of time together. One evening when we were presenting *Boy Scout* at the Albert Hall he asked me to meet after the performance a number of what he called "apprentices" whom he had invited to see the Pageant. I had no idea who or what these apprentices were and when I met them I discovered they were dressed in the uniform of the Royal Air Force, all of them young boys between the ages of fifteen and seventeen. They came in four coaches and

I was told they were R.A.F. apprentices stationed at Halton in Buckinghamshire. All would eventually become fully fledged airmen who had chosen the R.A.F. as their career. They were a tremendous bunch and we spent nearly an hour talking. A young Apprentice Sergeant, Peter Dunstan, did the introductions and we got along like a house on fire. Peter told me they had a Rover Crew on the Station and he invited me to come down and talk to them. I was delighted to accept and a few weeks later I paid my first visit to Halton.

It turned out to be an exciting night, for there I met a young boy who is still one of my closest friends, Johnny Brown. Mick Green was another boy I became firm friends with and we spent many holidays together when he was on leave. Mick was killed on V.J. night. My visits to Halton became more and more frequent; I attended their Passing Out Parades and several times I took some of the Arsenal football players down there on Sundays to play a game with their team. Cliff Bastin, Alex James and Eddy Hapgood were but three of those men who belonged to the great Arsenal team of those glory days and the Station Commander, Air Commodore Dacre (and as I discovered later a very intimate friend of Boyle), gave me every encouragement. We gave concerts for the apprentices and at every opportunity over to Halton I would go where I knew I would have a great time.

Major Boyle made his next move one night at a Gang Show. He came to me and told me he had a friend in a box whom he wanted me to meet during the interval. He took me up to the box and I met the man who immediately chatted to me as though he had known me for years. I realised he was not an Englishman and although Major Boyle had introduced me, his name meant nothing and I didn't even remember it. As far as I was concerned he could have been named "Smith." In that particular programme we had staged a burlesque item on keeping fit and the one thing I do remember him saying was, "I wish we could laugh at ourselves in my country about keeping fit as you appear to do."

Then within minutes he invited me to lunch. I thanked him and agreed, though I had not the slightest intention of going. Anyway, when we left the box and returned to the stage, Major Boyle told me he would like me to go to this lunch and that he would arrange a date. I had no idea at that moment that the man I had been talking to and who had invited me to lunch was the German Ambassador, Herr Ribbentrop! About three weeks later I had a phone call from Major Boyle giving me the date of the lunch which was to be at the old Holborn Restaurant in Kingsway.

Of course I went. Herr Ribbentrop had with him an elderly lady and a very blonde young boy about seventeen years old. I was still baffled as to why he was so keen on inviting me to this lunch (an excellent one incidentally) and the talk was only centred on the usual type of conversation which amounted to very little. We arrived at the coffee stage and then came a clue as to the real reason for the invitation. Ribbentrop asked if I would go as their guest to Germany to see the Hitler Youth Movement. "We'd like your opinion of the way we are running it, and with your experience of youth it could be most valuable." It took me a little by surprise and at the time I regarded it as a compliment. Then the boy (his name was Karl) took over. He certainly knew his job. He spoke excellent English and for at least a quarter of an hour talked without stopping. He told me about the terrific type of boy they had in the Hitler Youth Movement, and that I would be given a free hand to meet as many as I wished. He explained that it would be possible for me to live on one of their camps, thus meeting the boys on their home ground or, if I chose, I could live in an hotel or even with him and his family at his home. His enthusiasm impressed me – he obviously knew his subject inside out – and then he said, "If not at my home, at the homes of any other friends you may meet and would like to know better." These words did not at the time cause me to think of anything but his sincere hope of getting me to go to Germany, and I began to think it might be a very good idea and a change from my usual routine. However, I had just started rehearsing for a new Ivor Novello show at Drury Lane and I explained that such a trip could not be for at least several weeks. We shook hands and parted. I thanked them for the lunch and then Karl asked if he could send me some literature about the Hitler Youth Movement, so I gave him my address. He wrote to me at least six times and sent me a very handsome book filled with hand-picked photographs of boys in their various activities. The photographs were undoubtedly beautifully produced and they would have made an impression on anyone. But suddenly something in my mind clicked and I became suspicious – suspicious of what was really behind this pressing invitation.

I did not go to Germany, but for months after propaganda regularly came to me through the post, and on one occasion six of the Hitler Youth visited London and I met them and showed them round. I even had them to dinner at my home (I was still living in Norbury) and I was impressed with the way these boys had obviously been selected. They returned home after a two weeks' stay and each boy wrote to thank me for my interest whilst they were here and said that they hoped I would be coming to meet them again in Germany. I still did not go, and for that I shall for ever be thankful. However, I reported all these incidents in detail to Major Boyle. I remember his smiling as he said, "They play the game well and never miss a trick." What that meant I could only guess but I think I understood.

It was then 1938, and there started the genuine scare of a war ahead. Trenches were being dug here in the capital and rumours were rife. I was spending a week-end with Major Boyle and his wife at their home in Guildford; it was a Sunday and we were sitting on the lawn just after lunch. Mrs. Boyle suddenly appeared and said, "Archie, Adastral wants you." Now, I may be smart in some ways but I am particularly dumb in others and I thought "Adastral" was something to do with petrol. I asked Mrs. Boyle what "Adastral" was and to my surprise she said, "It's the Air Ministry where Archie works." Until then I hadn't the remotest idea that he worked at all so I asked what sort of work he did. Mrs. Boyle replied, "He's the D.D. of I." Not knowing what "D.D.I." could possibly stand for, I could only say, "*Is* he?" and then ask her. "Archie," she said, "Is the Deputy Director of Intelligence in the Royal Air Force." It shook me – why, I don't know, but it did – so when he came back from the telephone I went straight to the point and said, "Why did you never tell me you were in the Royal Air Force and a Deputy Director of Intelligence." He grinned and said, "I had no intention of telling you until the time was ripe." Said I, "When is the ripe time coming then?" He replied, "At this moment" and went on, "What will you do when the war comes?" Now this, as I have said, was 1938 and I, like many others, did not believe a war was possible and I told him so. I remember I kidded him and said, "You're like all the old Army men, you want to get on a horse, swing a sword and shout 'Charge'." He laughed, and then very seriously told me that though it might not come immediately war was a certainty. Then he added, "You didn't answer my question. What will you do when the war comes?" "I'd have to get 'in' " I replied, "All our boys would have to join up and what else could *I* do but join them." "That's all I wanted to hear" he said, "I want you to come in with me." "Doing *what*?" I asked. Back came the reply, "Exactly what I tell you to do." Now I was doing very well professionally at that time and I had no intention of exchanging my weekly pay packet for what I would be receiving in the Forces before I had to, and I told him this. He then explained that if I would do some studying about Intelligence with him and a colleague, he would see that I was not called up unless war was actually declared. The next week he took me along to the Air Ministry where I met the A.M.P., Lord Portal, who chatted to me and confirmed what Major Boyle had promised. So there and then began my introduction to the world of Secret Service.

Boyle had not yet told me the name of his colleague, but a dinner was arranged at a flat Boyle had in London where I would meet him and hear exactly why he had been so keen to get me into the R.A.F. I got one hell of a surprise when I walked into the flat. Boyle and his colleague were already there having a drink together, and to my amazement I saw that it was one of my top line Scouting pals. He had been Camp Chief at Gilwell for years, and I still regard him as the best they ever had. The man standing with Major Boyle was none other than J.S. (Belge) Wilson. One day a great book will be written about this man and his contribution not only to Scouting but to his country. One day an enterprising film producer will make a film of his remarkable achievements during the war years. Apparently he and Boyle had planned all along what they considered I could contribute to the war effort. We sat down and talked long into the night. The opening gambit came from Boyle. "Ralph, one of the main reasons I wanted you in with me is because whatever Station I send you to in any part of the world you would be bound to know some ex-Scouts or some ex-Halton apprentices. This could be more than useful, for they would know you and talk to you in quite a different way than they would to any other officer." The thing that moved me more than anything else that evening was to discover what an important position Belge Wilson occupied in the Intelligence hierarchy. Colonel Wilson will be remembered by many of the very senior members of the three Services for the fabulous things he planned and promoted during the Second World War.

It was decided that instead of going to the usual Intelligence Courses I would meet regularly with Major Boyle, and occasionally with Colonel Wilson, in the flat and go through the various things I had to know. I found it exciting and my enthusiasm knew no bounds. I also attended a course on the giving of Security Lectures and these, in fact,

I gave hundreds of times in every part of the globe during the war that eventually came. Sometimes I did three and four in a single day.

By the beginning of 1939 I was equipped with enough knowledge to appreciate what was expected of me, and throughout this period I was still closely in touch by mail with various members of the Hitler Youth Movement. Every letter, every book they sent me, was speedily delivered to Major Boyle.

The last week in August, as already mentioned, we had been playing at the Coventry Hippodrome and on our way back on that fatal Sunday morning we stopped at Bedford and bought a morning paper. The headline in the News of the World read, "Mussolini pleads for Peace." I turned to my friends with me and said, "There won't be a war!" At eleven o'clock that morning came Mr. Chamberlain's announcement. Prophecy has never been my strong point! It sure wasn't this time. The following week I donned the uniform of an R.A.F. Pilot Officer. Major Boyle had been promoted and was now Air Commodore Boyle, Director of Intelligence of the Royal Air Force.

I was placed under the personal supervision of a splendid man, Squadron Leader Calder, a Scot. He worked directly under Air Commodore Boyle and he knew of the long association between us. He constantly warned me to be careful when I spoke to the Air Commodore *always* to address him as "Sir." This wasn't as easy as it sounds because after so many years it was too easy to call him "Archie" and it would not have been too good if anyone heard a Pilot Officer calling an Air Commodore by his Christian name. I don't think I slipped up once but it came very near now and then. Going into town one night I met Ivor Novello and he said, "One thing about this war, Ralph, it gives you the let-out with Gang Shows." I agreed and I made up my mind that when the time came my sole consideration would be to get back to the professional theatre and completely drop my hobby. How was I to know then what lay ahead!

For the first three or four weeks I gave Security Lectures to the new officers and also to one or two local R.A.F. Stations. Our Headquarters was a school which had been taken over in Harrow and I was billeted in a house near by. Then I was ordered to return one evening for a meeting with the Air Commodore. I remember it was at nine o'clock, and when I entered his room Squadron Leader Calder was also there. He poured me out a drink and we sat down – all Service manners departed and we talked like three Scouters. Within minutes, the Air Commodore came to the point. He wanted me to go on a special job in France and he told me he and Calder had worked out what he termed "a very cunning little scheme." I was to go out with an ENSA Concert Party which would play in certain places directed by the Intelligence Department and I was to stay for four weeks playing in the show and, in between whiles, tackle the "special job" he wanted me to do. I admired this idea because it gave me a complete cover as an Intelligence Officer. Basil Dean (though he knew nothing about the main reason for my taking a party overseas) was delighted with the prospect of being able to use me so we met and got together about seven fairly well-known artistes and started rehearsing at Drury Lane, which was then the Headquarters of ENSA. It felt good to be back at the "Lane" and to be with show people again, and I was looking forward to the four weeks in France and in particular to carrying out my first "under cover" job for the Air Commodore and Calder. We had only been in rehearsal for three days when I was told by telephone to return to Harrow at once. We stopped the rehearsal and back I went wondering what was up. It didn't take long to find out. Air Commodore Boyle and Calder had been discussing my "mission" and they both decided it was too risky for me to go out on this expedition with people the Director didn't know. I reminded him that he didn't know *anyone* in show business and asked what he suggested. "Give me ten names of boys I know from the Gang Show" he said, "And you can take out a show with them." I quickly explained that all these chaps had jobs so were not available. He said: "That's not your worry. Just give me the names and leave the rest to me." Calder then chirped in with, "You will still go under the ENSA banner and you can call the Unit, "RALPH READER AND TEN BLOKES FROM THE GANG SHOW." My first thought was "There it is, once again, the 'Gang Show' " and then I realised it would only be for four weeks and, after all, what was four weeks? (Who could have foretold that those four weeks were going to mean five years and bring forth a name in that Second World War which will never be forgotten?)

Somehow (and how I never discovered) the ten chosen men were released from their civvy jobs and we got together and had a show ready within a fortnight. At one of our final rehearsals we had a never-to-be-forgotten experience. Suddenly the door opened and in came our King and Queen, King George VI and Queen Elizabeth (now the Queen Mother). Her Majesty smiled and said, "We've come to wish you God speed and good luck, Mr. Reader." She then shook hands with each member of the team and they both talked to us for about a quarter of an hour. Her Majesty took me aback when she suddenly said to me, "When did we first see your Gang Show?" I took a chance and guessed, "About four years ago I think, Mam." She shook her head and said, "Oh no, it was longer ago than that." She turned to the King and asked him the same question and he immediately replied, "It was six years ago." He was absolutely right. They were then of course the Duke and Duchess of York. The very night suddenly came back to me and I remembered that they had talked to the whole cast backstage after the performance. I spoke to one of the youngsters after they had gone and asked him what he thought of the Duchess. He said, "She's just like my Mum – only prettier."

Under the ENSA regime we were to depart for France one Sunday evening in November – the time of the "cold war" with London in the throes of the blackout. We were to leave from Victoria Station, and a dismal evening it was. Two other parties were also leaving with us, one headed by Leslie Henson and the other by Seymour Hicks. The date and time of our departure was *supposed* to be kept a secret but several friends of both the other parties (mostly relations I suppose) were there to see them off. When we got to Victoria Station the place looked jammed. Mums, dads, aunts, uncles, children and members of the Gang were filling every inch of the platforms. Some were crying (which made us feel like heroes going to the slaughter), others were slapping our backs and wishing us good luck, but without a smile on their faces, and every single member of our Unit began to think we were doomed men going away never to return. We eventually boarded the train, all cramming to look out of the windows to wave a final goodbye, and then the guard's whistle blew and in the darkness the train started to move out. At that moment something happened that I shall never forget. No cheers, no laughing, but with one accord the entire crowd of people standing watching the moving train started to sing, "We're riding along on the crest of a wave." I'd better leave it to your own imagination how we felt. It was a moment of heart-pulling that filled us with a pride rarely experienced. As we drew further and further away the singing became fainter and fainter until we heard it no more. That song has been sung thousands of times but never did it mean as much as on that November Sunday night when we pulled out of Victoria and gathered speed into the darkness of the night and an unknown destination. Leslie Henson stood near me and tears were rolling down his cheeks. I think most of us were shedding tears too but they couldn't be seen – they were inside. It was scarcely what you would call a happy journey to Folkestone and by the time we got there it was not only bitterly cold but pelting down with rain. However, we were greatly relieved when we saw the very fine hotel we were to spend the night at. At dawn next morning we were to board a ship to take us across the channel, but we were delayed for four days by the weather. They were the stormiest days I remember and we had to cool our heels as best we could. However, an oportunity came our way which gave us a chance to break the monotony. Half a dozen airmen were going on the same ship as we were and they too had been stranded in Folkestone so their officer asked if we could put on a little ad lib show for these lads. All our props were aboard the ship so everything had to be done without the aid of costumes or make-up. When the other two Units heard what we were planning to do they were determined not to be left out so they came in and bolstered up the cast. For those six airmen we did a performance with Leslie Henson, Tom Webster, Dorothy Ward, Binnie Hale, Sir Seymour Hicks, Violet Lorraine, a line-up of chorus girls and my own Unit. The hotel loaned us the ballroom and long before we had finished the first couple of items the ballroom was crowded by people who were staying in the hotel. They bought beer for the airmen who must have felt they were being given a Command Performance. Later that evening, Lord Rothermere arrived at the hotel, learned what we had done, and personally gave all the ladies who took part in the performance a box of chocolates and we had a bottle of champagne each and a cigar!

Five o'clock the next morning we were called. The weather had cleared and we were to sail at seven. The crossing was uneventful and Army lorries were waiting to take us to Arras where we met the lady who was the head of ENSA in France, a Madam Vernon. She had a splendid meal waiting for us and after we had eaten she gave us our instructions. Leslie's party was not to play that evening; Sir Seymour Hicks was due to give a performance in the Arras Theatre, and then Madam said, "Ralph, dear, you and your boys are going direct to the front line. You were supposed to give two shows there this evening but as the ship docked late they are trying to put as many as possible into the hall for one performance. Two motor-cycle escorts will travel with you to show you the way and you will stop for a moment at Lens and see where you are being billeted." Getting up at five in the morning, crossing the Channel and then driving to Arras had made us all feel tired, and now we learned that we were to give our first show about forty miles further on. We looked at each other somewhat ruefully and then one of the gang said, "Well, that's what we've come for isn't it?" It was, so we brightened up, collected our baskets with the props and costumes, loaded them into another Army truck, said goodbye to the other two ENSA shows and got aboard. Then following the two motor-cyclists we drove off to Lens and saw our billet. It was no palace!! In fact it was a dismal café with rooms above it and we wondered what those rooms had been used for prior to them being taken over by the military. We hadn't really any doubts, and we were not wrong either, but the café did have a bar which we quickly made use of before going on to Seclin where we were to give the show.

Whether anyone remembers that particular winter, I don't know, but when I tell you it was a cold one I am not exaggerating one bit. It was freezing, and the wind was blowing and cutting through our overcoats. As the miles clicked by we felt like doing anything but giving a show. When we arrived at the Town Hall in Seclin, however, dozens and dozens of empty lorries lined the streets and inside the hall hundreds of Army and R.A.F. men had been waiting hours for us. Their Entertainments Officer had been giving them a running commentary on our progress and by the time we got there, the excitement was electric. I walked on the stage just to let them know we had actually made it and the cheer that went up must have been heard way over in the German lines. As it subsided, a West Country voice shouted out to me, "How's Crewkerne?" Yes, one of my home-towners was sitting somewhere out front. I think it would be true to say that of all the thousands of shows we did during the next five years, not one was more moving than that initial performance. Afterwards, we went into at least a dozen different lorries loaded with the men returning to their various camps and they all wanted to shake our hands and thank us for coming. If ever these words are read by any man who was in the audience that night let me tell him now, WE WANTED TO THANK YOU!

Every night was a different experience. We played in barns, town halls, Nisson huts and once in a bakehouse, with the heat of the ovens cooking the next day's bread for the troops causing the make-up to roll off our faces. Remember, this was the period when there was no gun-fire, when nothing appeared to be happening, and each side stood by waiting for the first move. The lights were even full on at the frontiers and beyond. Our audiences varied, some nights there were hundreds and another night just a handful, but no matter how small the number we always gave them the entire show. I recall one night making an exit on a rigged-up stage – I opened a door and fell out in a field. In some of the larger halls, as it was such a bitter winter braziers were placed down the aisles, and though the smell was not too pleasant, at least they gave out a certain amount of warmth. Nine times out of ten the entire audience sat there in balaclavas, overcoats and gloves.

Through all this time I was giving Security Lectures and tackling the special mission the Air Commodore had sent me to try to accomplish. There was an enormous amount of subversive propaganda finding its way into some of the R.A.F. camps in the form of leaflets. We wanted to know the source of this supply and how it was getting into the barrack blocks and in to the hands of the troops. I was lucky and the foresight of the then "Major Boyle" and his talk with me that week-end in Guildford paid off. I am the first to admit that luck played the major part in my findings. Two ex-Halton apprentices and one ex-Scout put me on the trail. What I discovered I passed on immediately to my Senior Intelligence Officer in the Command and he then took over. I remember when I was leaving his office after I had given him the information I had gathered, he said, "What are you going to do when its all over, Reader? Back to the stage or to Scotland Yard?" We laughed, and he gave me a very welcome drink.

We were still at this house in Lens and in the backyard of the place they kept chickens, dozens of them, and they woke us up every morning at the crack of dawn with their crowing. It was bedlam, and as we seldom got back from any of the shows until well after midnight this didn't please us, so we decided the only way to get rid of this menace was to eat it, so for almost every meal we begged for "Poolay" (about the only French word we knew). We ate so many of those birds, it's surprising we didn't start laying eggs. Gradually the numbers lessened and the noise at dawn grew less and less until one happy morning we looked out and there were only six hens left. We took the plunge and asked for a special supper when we returned that night, certain that this would end our break-of-day chicken réveille. We finished them off and then had two bottles of champagne to celebrate. We could sleep the next morning in peace – SO WE THOUGHT! But at dawn there came the biggest chorus of cocks and hens splitting the ears of us all and when we jumped out of bed and looked into that yard, the old girl who ran the place had ordered another HUNDRED chicken! Fortunately, we were there only three more days and were then sent off to another billet several miles away. As we left the place we broke into song and to the tune of *Goodnight Ladies* sang "Goodbye Chicken." Next morning, when we woke in our new abode, TEN COWS GAVE US THE BIGGEST MOOING CHORUS I HAVE EVER HEARD. We gave up – after all, we couldn't start eating a cow apiece.

I had an interesting experience when we were sent suddenly to Rheims and billeted at the Lion D'or Hotel, a top-class establishment which was a mighty big change from some of the dumps we had previously stayed in. One morning I was sitting in the lounge of the hotel and in came a man who checked in his hat with the girl at the counter. Then he walked to the bar, ordered a drink which he drank straight back, and then returned for his hat. Now this struck me as strange. If he only wanted a 'quickie' I couldn't understand why he should have checked in his hat. I waited for three days to see if he would return and he did. The same routine – hat checked, a quick drink, then a tip for the girl and out he went. To me it didn't make sense, so I reported the incident to the Intelligence Department and as far as I was concerned that was my part of the job done. I had frequently reported all sorts of completely innocent happenings which turned out to be nothing at all. I did not know the result of this tip off I gave about the man, the drink, and the hat, until I read a book long after the war and discovered that the hat-check girl was passing on information she gathered from the various members of the Services who frequented the bar by inserting it in the rim of the hat. I read then that she had been arrested and, so the story goes, she was found to be on the other side and was shot. One seldom knows the results of any reports one sends in because it is usual for an Intelligence Officer to go only from "A" to "B" and then someone else takes over. A wise plan this, because should anyone fall into enemy hands he would know only the smallest part of any investigation and would therefore have little to contribute under interrogation.

On Christmas Day we played in a barn and performed on a made-up stage. In addition to the usual audience we had horses, cows and goats neighing and mooing and bleating throughout the performance. It wasn't a particularly happy Christmas for us but one bright thing did happen. On Christmas Eve we had our very first mail from home and no letters we have ever had meant as much to us as those that awaited us when we arrived at yet another new billet on the night before Christmas. A very dear lady had sent me a Christmas pudding from England which we had carried around with us for some time. We handed it, with instructions, to the woman in charge of the billet, but when at the end of the meal the long awaited moment arrived and she brought it in, she had *baked* it and it was the size of a small bun. We stared at it in frustration and then one of the gang grabbed hold of a bottle of brandy and poured the lot over the mess and lit it. We nearly blew the roof off the room and the pudding practically exploded, but we ate it, just a nibble each, and drank the brandy, which we managed to blow out in time to prevent the woman from throwing a bucket of water over the blaze. I look back on that Christmas as one of the worst I have ever spent. We just sat around and read and re-read those wonderful letters from HOME.

Reports had been sent back to England about the success of the performances we were giving and because of this our tour was extended another four weeks.

Madam Vernon came to see us, congratulated us on our job and gave us a night in Paris before we went on to another destination. Paris! As the theatres were still open there, we all went to the Casino where Josephine Baker and Maurice Chevalier were playing. A great show, and then we parted, each saying he was going to explore the city. I was dead beat and decided to go straight back to the hotel, though I didn't tell any of the boys. Imagine my surprise when I arrived there to find that every single one of the gang had done the same thing. Paris saw nothing of us that night. Our journeys, the work and the constant changes had taken their toll so we just returned to the hotel and went to bed. Next morning we took the train to another base. Those four extra weeks passed without event and then came the time to return home. I to go back to Harrow and my Service job, the remainder of the gang back to their civilian jobs. So ended that first tour of the Second World War and I salute right here and now every bloke who shared it with me. They were all Scouts and through all the difficulties they never complained – yes, they were indeed great Scouts.

My next assignment had been arranged some time before

I got back and within an hour after reporting at Harrow, Squadron Leader Calder told me what it was to be. It was quite different from anything I had expected. The Poles had been arriving from Poland and were being stationed at Eastchurch where they were to be formed into a Polish Air Force. The Station was under the command of Group Captain Davidson – a splendid officer I was proud to serve under. Air Commodore Boyle filled me in with details as to what I was to do. "Keep them occupied and keep them happy" he told me, "That's all you have to do." That's all!! I couldn't speak a word of Polish and I guessed very few of them would know a single word of English. To cap it all, there were only about 150 British airmen on the Station – the Poles numbered about two thousand. Some odds. I duly reported to the Station Commander and he gave me a free hand. My first thought was to arrange football matches and this meant recruiting practically every British man on the Station. Knowing the hardships the Poles had been through, I thought we could at least hold our own. Some hopes! Those Polish lads went into every match as though it were an International, and within a quarter of an hour of each game we were losing by three to four goals. I quickly switched to boxing. This turned out even worse, for hardly any of our own boys managed to stay on their feet after the first or second round. To say I was despondent is putting it mildly, but suddenly came a break-through.

One morning as I was passing the NAAFI, I heard the sound of men singing and the singing was far from ordinary; in fact it was some of the most beautiful music I have ever heard. I stood outside and listened and then I went in. The NAAFI had been decorated with hundreds of various paper designs in vivid colours and in the most artistic way. At least two hundred voices were singing songs of their Polish homeland and this gave me an idea. I would put on a gigantic concert. We employed over a hundred of the Poles to erect a stage in a hangar and the zeal with which they undertook this task was exciting to watch. Then we used about 300 of them in the show and approximately a couple of dozen of our own lads. Fortunately there was a Polish Count who spoke perfect English and when I explained the idea to him he was right with me. The plan was that I would compere the show, telling jokes, etc., and he would translate each one into Polish. If anyone doubted that a miracle could happen he would have been re-assured if he had been in the audience the night of that concert. What the Count was saying when he explained my gags I don't know, but they brought the house down. The night turned out to be a triumph and a party was given afterwards which lasted well into the next morning. Naturally we had to repeat the show and they clamoured for another and then another.

We were all very amused by the way in which the Poles took care of their hair. At night they even wore nets and various clips, etc., to keep it in place. So far as they were concerned it was their normal custom and perfectly natural and they would arrive at rehearsals with these adornments on their heads without the slightest sign of embarrassment. Fortunately, we became quite used to the sight after a few days.

During rehearsals I taught them to say a slang word I have often used when things go well – "Chickedy-Snitch." The Count explained what this meant and every minute of the day and night you would hear somebody shout out, "Chickedy-Snitch." It really caught on and months later when I had a chance to come to London and visit a theatre, as I walked to my seat there was a loud shout from somewhere up in the balcony when two or three Poles who were also attending the show saw me and shouted out, "Chickedy-Snitch." The audience broke into a roar of laughter as I turned around and waved to the lads upstairs.

At one of the shows we did at Eastchurch some of the Brass Hats from the Air Ministry came down to see us and were so enthusiastic that they suggested we should take the performance to the big local cinema in Sheerness for two Sunday performances, when they would invite some of the local people who had been so helpful to our Allies when they visited the town, because it would help with good relationships. They also agreed it would be good to bring down some of the very Senior Officers from Poland who were stationed at the Air Ministry in London. This came about and among them they brought General Sikorski. The General was so impressed, not merely with the presentation, but with the way the Poles and the Britishers were working together, that in the Mess afterwards he even told me in so many words that I might become the next President of Poland! Not only was he somewhat taken aback by the success of this Service entertainment, but so were the high-ranking officers from our own Air Ministry, and within a week I was called to London for a conference.

They explained to me that entertainment was going to play a vital part in the war and they asked me to form a small unit of airmen who could visit outlying stations all over the country and give shows for them. In other words it was to be a re-creation of the outfit we had taken to France, but this time the unit would be made up of serving men. "We'll have our own Gang Show Unit" I was told and we can call it the "R.A.F. Gang Show." They explained to me that I would still be working under instructions from Air Commodore Boyle but that I would also be handling this Entertainment Unit. Now came the task of recruiting suitable airmen and to the rescue came some of the old Scout Gang who did the French tour. Within a fortnight, Jack Beet, George Cameron, Jack Healy, Eric Christmas and later Bill Sutton 'signed on' and went straight into training on the Barrack Square at Uxbridge. This was, of course, essential before transfer to the Entertainment Unit. With a few additional volunteers the very first "R.A.F. Gang Show" was formed within a month and during the time the lads were doing their training I spent every waking hour writing material and songs for this new venture. At the back of my mind came the realisation that the Gang Show was around my neck once again and there was no disguising the fact that I was stuck with it.

There were teething troubles, one in particular. I somehow hated the thought of so many of my old mates having to call me "Sir" and they obviously couldn't address me as "Ralph" in the presence of other officers, so it was decided to call me "Chief", and this title has stuck to this very day. Our opening performance was a riot. I had written material that *belonged* to the airmen and the services and every joke simply wowed them and the odd bits of sentiment were just enough to give the show a change of pace. We had plenty of difficulties, arriving at various stations at all hours of the day and night, so that the question of meals became a problem, but somehow we got over it. Within three months we had created such a name in the R.A.F. that the Air Ministry decided they needed more Units. So I toured around looking for enough talent to form three more R.A.F. Gang Shows. Luckily in St. Athen I discovered Reg Dixon, who later became one of our top comedians and a fine professional – he was one of our worthiest members. In fact he took charge of the first of the three Units we formed. Now this meant the Air Ministry had to form an Establishment for the growing Units and we badly needed an experienced man who knew the Rules and Regulations of the Royal Air Force. Here again we struck oil. Visiting one night the R.A.F. Station at Hornchurch, during the meal they provided us with prior to the show I was surprised to hear Scout Gang Show records being played. I spoke to a young Corporal, Frank Plummer, and asked him where the records had come from and he told me that Flight Sergeant Cracknell (who incidentally had been an ex-Halton apprentice) was also a keen Scout, so I talked to him. It was obvious Jack would be a perfect choice to handle the new Establishment as he, being a Regular, knew many people at Records and this I recognised would be a very important asset. Air Marshals might be very powerful, but no-one could wangle things in a more subtle way than a friendly Warrant Officer. Jack Cracknell knew dozens of these men and I immediately set to work to get him into our outfit. I had a little difficulty with some of the old Gangsters and we had many arguments but eventually I won the day and Flight Sergeant Cracknell was posted from Hornchurch to become a Pilot Officer in the Establishment of the R.A.F. Gang Shows. There is no use dodging the issue, he pulled more "strings" than anyone else I know in order to get the men I needed, even going over the heads of many very senior officers. We had opposition at times, but somehow Jack got over it, and soon there was an order to increase the three Units to six!

Here I must explain that we were only allowed to recruit men known as A.C.H.(G.D.)s, the lowest paid members in the R.A.F., so off I went round the stations on the search for more "Entertainers." We were not allowed to touch any Tradesmen so we were limited as to whom we could approach. But our luck held. One day I met a young airman who told me he played the drums. I asked him if there was anything else he could do and he said, "Well I can do a few impersonations." I told him to report to the NAAFI next morning and I would see what he could do. When I arrived at the appointed time, I heard 'myself' singing (even worse than I do) *We're riding along on the crest of a wave*. I walked on the stage *BEHIND* the impersonator, who didn't see me, but a few of the airmen who were supposed to be cleaning out the NAAFI were sitting on chairs enjoying the airman's performance. The moment they saw me they stood up and the singer turned around. He saluted and said, "Sir! Do I get 'jankers' or are you thirsty?" His name? Peter Sellers. He didn't get 'jankers' but we did have a drink and Peter became a member of the Establishment. Another discovery was Dick Emery and Dick has been one of the most loyal men I have ever met and is, today, one of the best known and loved comedians in the country. He still never misses an opportunity to tell of the experience he got whilst he was with me. Thanks, Dick! Dear Tony Hancock was another we found and I have a quote from a magazine in which he wrote, "I remember Reader's encouragement with warmth and gratitude. He turned me from a raw amateur into something approaching a professional." What a loss it was to the world of the theatre when Tony left us. Television has not yet discovered another Hancock.

From six Units we went to twelve and from these other Units came the names of such brilliant men as Norrie Paramor, Cardew Robinson, Harry Worth, the Cox Twins, Graham Stark and many others too numerous to mention. But their names are in the Royal Air Force records and there they will remain for all time.

As I have said I was still working for Air Commodore Boyle during this period and I well remember one ticklish assignment he landed me with. Trailing a suspected Fifth Columnist (and the suspicion turned out to be correct) proved an interesting experience as the man concerned was working along lines exactly similar to my own. He was a member of an amateur concert party entertaining the troops on various stations and was collecting a lot of very useful information. However, it is not so much about the particular incident itself I want to tell you, but the fact that the job happened to take me to the R.A.F. Station, Bramcote, which is not far from Coventry, and passing through that city I saw the playbills of the Hippodrome and discovered that a pal of mine was playing there that week. As my old Commanding Officer from Eastchurch, Group Captain Davidson, was now in charge at Bramcote I felt sure I could get the night off, so I booked two seats for the Hippodrome and then booked a room in an hotel for the night. However, when I arrived at Bramcote and reported to the Group Captain he explained that he had a special appointment that evening and wanted me to escort his wife to a cocktail party in the Mess. I was disappointed at not being able to get to the Hippodrome, but obviously had to do as I was told. Lucky me! It was the night of that devastating air-raid on Coventry and the hotel I would have been staying in was completely destroyed.

I had long wanted to have girls in the R.A.F. Gang Show Units, but the Air Ministry at first would not approve, so I suggested we formed two WAAF Units and this they agreed to. We called them the Number One and Number Two WAAF Gang Show Girls and what girls they turned out to be. Never a murmur about the sometimes tough conditions they had to work under and the miles they travelled. Especially do I remember just after "D" Day, when they were sent to Normandy and bravely stood up to all the fighting that surrounded them with never a complaint. I cannot mention them all, but Sgt. Molly Watson in charge of the Number One Unit was a *tour de force* when things became difficult. If I mention Queenie Isaacs, it's because she has since done such wonderful work with the Association we formed after the war ended – and I'd like to mention not only Queenie but every single girl who brought such joy and glamour to the fighting men of the Services.

We ultimately had 25 Units touring all over the world and giving shows to the Troops, from the Eighth Army in the Desert to the Burma boys fighting the Japs. No battle front was missed and the loyalty these girls and men gave is something I cannot fully describe. During all this time I tried to stay as long as possible with my own Unit but I did manage to keep in constant touch with all the others. Throughout the war the longest leave I took was 48 hours. This was entirely my own fault. The moment my own Unit went on leave I chased around to see the others as I was detemined to keep the whole Establishment together as a family and that is exactly what we were, and what we still are.

I've already mentioned our going overseas, and to cover this I think it is time to start another chapter.

11

The Royal Air Force and World War Two: Part 2

As with anything that is successful, not a few people tried to have a finger in the Gang Show pie. Great efforts were made to dabble in and reconstruct the R.A.F. shows but we were a closed shop. Thanks to my position with Air Commodore Boyle and the great support I received from the Director of Air Force Welfare, Air Commodore Strang Graham, we soon overcame any interference.

We knew that the Gang Shows would soon be drafted overseas and it was no surprise when the Director sent for me one morning and told me I should be leaving for 'the other side' very shortly. One of the Units was to go with me. The first trip would be made by sea and we were to leave for West Africa and make our way from there to the Middle East.

Montgomery had already started his guns booming at El Alamein and the plan was for us to join up with the Eighth Army as soon as possible. It was exciting to think we were off to join the boys who were really doing the job.

I well remember walking on to the ship the day we were

due to sail. I arrived early and a young corporal was standing at the top of the gangway awaiting the arrival of the officers and I happened to be about the first. He said to me, when I had given him my name, "O.K. sir, you've got a single cabin." I said, "Thank God" and then he added, "With six others." It was so cramped that we could only dress one at a time.

It was a long voyage but certainly not a boring one. I was in charge of the entertainments and sports on board and every night we had something on the agenda. I also had to censor the letters of the R.A.F. personnel. I recall one line in a letter a chap was writing to his mother. "Ralph Reader is on board," he wrote, "Please tell Grandfather, as I expect he will remember him in the last war." I don't know how old that young man thought I was, but he was wrong!

One night a couple of youngsters asked me to help them organise a whist-drive. The trouble was there were not enough playing cards, and the naval officer concerned didn't seem too anxious to help. When I spoke to him, the officer explained that if he lent us his precious packs of cards the players would inevitably pocket them – with the result that there would be none left for the return trip. I must say I saw the force of his argument! Would I be responsible, he asked? I promised that however many packs he lent the lads, they would be returned, and he gave in.

Alas, at the end of the game, fourteen packs were missing. Next morning I called the men together and told them that I wanted those fourteen packs returned. I emphasised that I didn't care who took them, that I didn't want to know. I would put a basket on deck that night and during the darkness it was up to those fourteen blokes to return the packs of cards. They did, and when we counted the number of packs found in the basket next day, they numbered twenty-three!

In Freetown, where the convoy stayed for four days, the Gang put on shows for all the local R.A.F. Stations. The first man I met outside an orderly room was a Scouter from Scout

Headquarters in London, and wherever we went there were friends waiting for us. Halls were packed to suffocation half an hour before the curtain was due to go up and the heat was almost unbearable. Greasepaint melted all over the dressing-tables and even when we tried keeping the sticks in water until we needed them, it wasn't enough to prevent them from softening. Nor had we bargained for the utter impossibility of making a quick change from a dress soaked in perspiration. The costumes stuck to the body and just wouldn't budge, and because of this, cue after cue was missed at the first performance we gave in Freetown. A new routine had to be worked out to give the female impersonators more time to change, and this experience of giving shows in the heat was to be of great value to us during the months ahead.

From Freetown we sailed on to Takaradi, where the Commanding Officer, having heard of my interest in football, had arranged a match by the Station team against a local West African side. I had never before seen players kicking the ball without boots, so for the first few moments I shuddered every time a bare foot caught a ball. But the way those natives controlled and passed and eventually hit a dead football was something I shall always remember.

At Takaradi was a telegram with instructions to leave the Unit and report immediately to Cairo, so I said goodbye to the lads, boarded a plane and headed for Egypt. Next day I was taken to Headquarters and had only been there a few moments when an orderly came to tell me that an R.A.F. sergeant was waiting to see me. To my great delight the sergeant was Mick Green. I have already mentioned him earlier but let me just tell you a little more about him.

Mick and I first met when he was a sixteen-year old apprentice at Halton and from our first meeting we became pals. Mick was a well-built, tallish youngster, with fair hair, clear eyes and just about the most honest smile a fellow ever had. To him, the Royal Air Force was the finest career in the world and he was very proud of being an ex-Brat. A week never went by without a letter from him. Eventually his overseas posting came through and until this meeting in Cairo I hadn't seen him for a couple of years. So it is easy to imagine my delight when he walked into the Welfare Office the day after I had arrived in the Middle East. I remember a Group Captain saying on one occasion, "Reader, your young sergeant is outside, what a great advertisement he is for the R.A.F." No airman took more pride in his appearance than Mick and I was extremely proud of that officer's words. The last thing Mick talked to me about was a holiday in England on his next leave. He didn't come home. The night the R.A.F. Pageant opened at the Albert Hall, a large parcel came to me from a Padre in the Middle East. In it I found every letter I had ever sent to Mick. A brief note was inside on which the Padre had written, "I think you might like to know what this grand boy thought of you. I shall miss him too." He was twenty-three. So long, Mick.

The Unit had now arrived in Cairo and our instructions were to leave at the earliest moment for Tripoli, where we would pick up a couple of lorries and then head straight for the desert and the Eighth Army. Group Captain Stubbs, in charge of Middle East Welfare, was very anxious for us to give a show in Cairo before we left, so the night before (which happened to be a Sunday) a special performance was planned for the theatre there. It was to be a gala night, in the presence of Air Chief Marshal Sholto Douglas, Admiral Cunningham and King Farouk. Unwisely, they did not issue tickets, merely advertising the time of the performance. Thousands wanted to see the show and the streets around that theatre were completely blocked. The boys and I couldn't even get near the stage door, and it looked almost as if there would be no performance. The day was saved by a troop of Egyptian Scouts, helped by the Egyptian police.

We were nearly an hour late kicking off for that show. Even the Brass-hats couldn't get through the seething mob. Inside, we had put the orchestra on the stage to make room for more men, and the orchestra pit was jammed tight with every type of serviceman. Boxes for four and six people were holding anything from twelve to twenty, and the aisles of the theatre had completely disappeared, for men were sitting on the floor, upstairs and down. It was nearly one o'clock in the morning before we rang down and we left for Tripoli by plane at day-break.

When the kite came to pick us up I got aboard and made my way to the gun-turret in the nose of the plane. It looked about the best spot to me, so I staked my claim, but strangely enough I didn't sleep at all. After we had taken off we suddenly discovered one of the Gang had been left below, and that shook us quite a bit. Then, after getting myself comfortably set in my turret, I had an idea for a song and began to write it.

By the time we arrived at Castel Benito I had written a number that was as popular as any song we sang to the troops on that tour. It was *A Sunny Day,* a number I used to do as an airman writing a letter home to his wife, and reading aloud one of her letters he had just received. It was a sentimental sort of thing but in those days it just fitted the mood of all of us over there. Hundreds of blokes wrote to me for copies of that lyric.

From Tripoli, across the desert, we travelled in two trucks, which we used for sleeping, for dressing rooms and even stages. On and on we went, stopping whenever we felt like it to brew 'char' and then tackling the remaining miles for the show that night. We were as brown as Indians, never more healthy, except for an occasional attack of 'gyppy tummy' and, quite frankly, enjoying ourselves. Sometimes we would be playing to thousands, at other times to a mere handful. Once we pulled up at a water-hole where about a dozen men were stationed. When they said they hadn't seen a show since they left England, we told them they were going to see one right away. We got out the props, rigged up the stage and did a complete programme for those boys, eventually camping there for the night. They found some beer, we pooled some of our 'extras', and round a camp fire that evening we talked of home as only those far away in a foreign land can do. We left early next morning and as long as we were in view we looked back to see those boys still waving to us.

Tunis was ahead, and there we camped with the South Africans. I shared a tent with their Padre. By my bedside I always kept a book given me by the Scouts from the Albert Hall show and each of the fifteen hundred boys in that Pageant had signed his name in it. Returning to the tent one Sunday evening I found a note from the Padre, "Dear Reader, I am away for a few days and shall not be back before you leave. I looked at your book and found my young brother's signature in it. Give him my love when you return to England, yours, Richardson." It's a small world.

In some ways, our roving assignment in the desert must have been one of the strangest in the story of the war. We worked to a plan – but only up to a point. We gave shows at our own discretion and were, to all intents and purposes, strolling players in uniform. Our life was an extraordinary mixture – it was both Bohemian and disciplined. Sometimes we were lonely, especially at night when on our way to catch up with advancing units. We would drop in on native villages and go rat-catching with the inhabitants. And everywhere – as all who fought in Africa will remember – you would meet a couple of natives selling eggs. You could have sworn there was not a soul in sight, and then these odd-looking merchants would appear as suddenly as though from some trap-door in the sandy expanse.

We played to every sort of audience, comprising men from every spot in the world, and whether they understood a word we were saying or not. The coloured troops in particular were quite uproarious, for when they saw some of my chaps dressed up in feminine clothes, they threw themselves on the ground in a delirium of laughter. We all feared they would have fits, and the sound of their hilarious guffaws was something out of this world. It ruined the timing of the lines but certainly added to the entertainment.

The worst part of this trip were the morning performances. Being up late, travelling along tracks that cut the speed down to about seven miles an hour and being shaken from side to side in the lorries didn't help, and after that to rise early in the morning and attempt to be funny at ten o'clock required more than an ordinary effort. Luckily, the audiences didn't seem to worry, so we got along quite well. I vowed I would never again go to Margate, for I never wanted to see another grain of sand *ever*. Sand was in our ears, our eyes, our hair, and no matter how we tried to wash it out there was always a supply left. The costumes were standing up to things surprisingly well, but now and again some of them would give up the ghost and fall to pieces. There was no hope of getting fresh supplies, and by the time the tour was ended we were using one dress for about eight scenes. It was an experience worth enduring, but not one I'm anxious to tackle again. For one thing, the memory of those lonely crosses marking the graves of British and German soldiers alongside the desert tracks I shall always carry with me.

The tour completed, we turned again towards Tripoli and the thought of getting back there and being able to sleep in a bed with sheets was something to be dreamed about. Every mile seemed like ten. None of us had shaved for about three days and we must have looked pretty awful. As we entered the town, the first thing I saw was a poster of a show playing there – *Spring Party* with Leslie Henson, Vivien Leigh, Dorothy Dickson and Beatrice Lillie. I could hardly believe my eyes. I shouted to Jock, our driver, "Get to the theatre right away," and in a few minutes the lorry pulled up at the stage door. I rushed in (what I must have looked like I dare not think) and standing before me in the most beautiful white evening gown was Vivien Leigh. After those weeks in the desert, the sudden sight of this lovely English girl was a vision I shall never forget. Leslie, in that husky voice of his, said, "And what, pray, are *you* made up for?" He laughed as he looked at me, three days' growth on my chin, a pair of shorts nearly up to my waist and an old shirt with half the collar torn away. But it didn't matter. It was a reunion and a reunion in those days was something to make a fuss about.

That night at the Officers' Club, I looked at the beautiful bed and the clean sheets and thought there could be no prettier sight this side of heaven. I went to bed early and lay there breathing a sigh of contentment – for about ten minutes. Then I had to get up. A million insects were crawling all over me, so I had to sleep for the rest of the night in a chair in the lobby! The next morning I went over to the Union Theatre where my boys were. They had been given beds in a very large dressing room and when I walked in they were still sleeping. The first man who woke up, looked at me and said, "You and your Officers' Club! I bet you had sheets and slept like a blooming king." I just couldn't tell him the truth.

From Tripoli we went back to Cairo where our plans had already been settled for the following months. The Unit was to move on without me. I was to stay in Cairo until I had formed three parties with local men and then a long trip had been fixed for me on my own. I can't say this appealed to me. The prospect of travelling thousands of miles through half-a-dozen different countries wasn't my idea of a picnic but I could do nothing about it. I made up my mind that whatever else happened, I was going to enjoy those last few weeks in Cairo.

This was easy. Alice Delysia was there and so was Constance Carpenter, while to top it all, Jack Benny pulled in just after I arrived. We gave several concerts together. Jack and I went back over the days long ago at the Palace in New York and Connie took me to the night-spots. I remember on one occasion how I bragged to Connie that I knew King Farouk. In a sense this was true because when he was fourteen years old he came to see *Boy Scout* as he was at the time Chief Scout of Egypt. I had lunch with him during his stay in London and one of his entourage told me that if I ever came to Cairo I should call on them. The idea of my ever being in Cairo was remote to say the least, but here I was right in the centre of it. So I shot a line to Connie that I *knew* the King. The end of the story was that I rang the Palace (owing to the refreshment we had taken – it was after midnight anyway) and lo and behold, three days later Group Captain Stubbs came to me and said, "Reader, what's this about an invitation to the Palace?" I was scared to death, never dreaming that the message I had given over the phone that night would be taken seriously. But it was, and I went! It was quite an experience! We drank tea, although how I drank it I don't know because I hate sugar and this tea was nothing but syrup. His Majesty was with us for only a few minutes but the incident has become another of those unforgettable memories and just goes to show what Scouting can do for you!

Noel Coward arrived and Cairo began to look like the West End of London. Then came a summons for us to report to Alexandria. The British Fleet were bringing in the surrendered Italian Fleet and we were sent to the port to report to the naval authorities and give shows aboard the various ships anchored in the harbour.

As we boarded the flagship, a guard of honour met us and the Captain told me he wished me to meet personally each member of the guard. They had all been selected from ex-Scouts and Rovers in the ship. Only the Navy could have thought of that one. For the next ten days we played our show aboard every ship there was – cruisers, battleships and destroyers, even a couple of dredgers. During a performance on H.M.S. King George V the air-raid alarm sounded. Everybody went instantly to action stations and our boys were sent below. Jack Beet dressed as a Principal Boy in scarlet padded tights, sliding down ladders amid very nautical wisecracks from the sailors was a sight not to be missed. The alarm proved false, and within a matter of minutes we were back on the stage carrying on. Ten minutes later, a very young middy was sent to me by the Captain to apologise for the interruption. Apparently, it was his fault the alarm had sounded. The kid was very embarrassed and stammered out his regrets, but I tried to put him at his ease and in a couple of minutes, I'm glad to say, he was calling me "Ralph."

I spent a weekend at the British Embassy and just couldn't resist the opportunity of writing letters to all my friends at home on the official notepaper.

One evening at a bar I had just ordered a round when a matelot behind me put some money on the counter. As I turned to protest, he said, "No Gang Show bloke is going to pay for drinks when a K.G. Five man is around." Such is the hospitality of the Navy. When we left, as the pinnace drew away from the battleships the entire fleet seemed to be sending us on our way.

Then Cairo again, more farewells, and at last my journey to India began. I went by seaplane, a luxurious boat with every conceivable comfort for passengers. Most of the passengers were civilians and one man in particular gave us quite a lot of amusement. For some reason or other, he never spoke a word. Now it so happened that about twice a day the plane landed on the water and a British Airways pinnace invariably came alongside to take us off for refreshments on shore. Each pinnace was of the same colour and design and manned always by the same number of men dressed in white uniforms. On the third day's travel, the silent man spoke for the first time. We had landed, the door had opened and straight in front of the opening was the usual pinnace. The dumb gentleman just looked and, as though to himself, said, "That ruddy boat always gets here ahead of us!"

We touched down at Karachi, where I made rapid plans to visit many units, put new ideas into their own parties and appear myself as a guest performer. Again, a poster gave me news of an old friend. "Karachi Follies, with Johnny Rew," I read. It was "Dink" Rew all right, and our reunion seemed a good omen for my Indian tour.

Delhi was the real starting point of a pretty gruelling trip which took in Calcutta, Chittagong and then Burma. Week after week I battered my way along, giving three or four shows a day,working with Station concert parties, giving lectures and generally making myself useful. One night I had to go to a small squadron in the advanced area but I didn't arrive until one in the morning. When I got there, they were having a sing-song in a small Basha hut, the only illumination being an old hurricane lamp hanging from the ceiling. There was no stage, so I just jumped on a chair and got cracking with jokes and songs. After a while I called for a volunteer to carry on while I had a break. A youngster got up and said he could tell some stories, so I said, "All right, son, get busy while I have a smoke." I lit a cigarette and went outside, into the thick, filthily heavy jungle night. I could dimly make out a hundred men sitting on the floor in the smoke-filled hut, by the faint light of the old oil lamp. It looked like the end of the world and worse than the black hole of Calcutta. Suddenly, a young airman was standing by me. I said "Hello" to him. Then very simply, he said to me, "You know, sir, this is all very wonderful to me. I've never been backstage before." I'm always sorry I didn't ask that chap his name.

The airmen were getting far too little entertainment, some of them absolutely none, and I was determined to try to get parties out to them. I sent signal after signal to the Air Ministry but they had far too much on their plate to be able to reply. I then did all I could to form local parties to visit the isolated units, but again permission had to be obtained from Headquarters for this and somehow it got stuck in the "pending" file, and that was that.

The Gang Show Unit I had left in Cairo was on its way but it would be weeks before they could get to Burma and in any case how could one party cover so many thousands of miles? I tried every trick I could think of to enlist the help of the Commanding Officers: but though they were sympathetic they could do little without the O.K. from the top, and this I just couldn't get.

Letter after letter was sent to the Welfare Directorate at home but without result. I became more and more discouraged. It seemed quite wrong to me that at home and on the big stations near bases, visiting stars would stay for days, while the lads who were really in the wilds had nothing. I flew back to Calcutta in desperation and then on to Delhi, but in spite of promises I returned to Burma feeling I was fighting a losing battle. Weeks went by, and still no word from the Air Ministry. I was sure they had forgotten me completely and that I should end my days in the jungle. But the spirit of the boys in that hellish country was beyond praise and if I had to be lost I couldn't have chosen finer companions. I never gave up sending signals nor writing letters, but for all the good they did they might have been written in sand.

At last one Wing Commander in Burma said to me out of the blue, "Ralph, I'll take a chance. If you can find half a dozen men in my command who could be moulded into a show I'll let you have them." In the next few days I must have auditioned nearly every man in that area, but I got hold of the chaps I wanted. They weren't brilliant, but they were enthusiastic and that was enough for me. I worked those men like slaves, hardly stopping for meals, and in three days I had begun to take the rough edges off them. At last here was something to send out to the blokes in the wilds. Then came what looked like a knock-out blow. It was a signal from the Air Ministry. "Reader to report immediately to C. in C. North Africa Command. This cannot be altered."

My Commanding Officer in Chittagong tried to cheer me up. "You are going to meet one of the really great men, Reader," he said. "You'll be meeting Tedder." I'm afraid I couldn't enthuse very much about this; all I could understand was that I couldn't get that show through to the 'erks.' The C.O. went on, "If you can have a heart-to-heart chat with Tedder you'll find that he will understand everything you are trying to do. Remember that all the way over there. He'll understand."

From that time onwards, through the long flying hours with Burma, India, Egypt skidding along beneath me, all I could think of was, "A heart-to-heart talk... he'll understand...he's a great man..." But *how* could I have a heart-to-heart talk? I was only a Squadron Leader, I could hardly pull out a cigarette case, offer it to an Air Marshal, and expect him to listen to *my* worries. I tried to rehearse my first speech to him. I even wrote out a script and memorised it. By the time we reached Algiers, I was a nervous wreck.

As I walked into Wing Commander Scarman's office he handed me a telegram. It was from the boys I had left several days before in Chittagong. "Do your best, sir, we are counting on you and so are the rest of the lads." I had that funny feeling in my stomach that you only get when you feel you are batting against *all* odds. Then the Wing Commander spoke. "Sit down, Ralph." That was a good start. I sat, he pulled out a packet of cigarettes and offered me one, and that was even better.

Nervously I tried to tell Scarman of the frustration and helplessness of my position and how difficult I was finding it to get entertainment to the men who really needed it. "When you meet the Chief," Scarman told me, "Talk to him just as you have been talking to me. He'll understand." There it was again, "He'll understand."

I put on shows all over and around Algiers while waiting for the summons to the Chief's Headquarters. On Christmas Day, 1943, I did seven, and to my great delight at one of the performances there in the audience was one of my Units straight from England. They had just landed, heard I was on the job, and got permission to come along. What a reunion!

Unexpectedly, the Chief's personal plane was sent

for me. I left Algiers for Tunis that morning as though I was going to my execution. We touched down half way there and picked up a passenger, Randolph Churchill. He was on his way to see his father who was ill with pneumonia. Then, below us was Tunis, drenched in rain. By a great stroke of luck I recognised the Group Captain waiting for me. Usually I am hopeless at remembering faces, but Group Captain McGregor had married a girl from my home-town and only a few months before I had been on his station at Tangmere. I thanked him for coming to meet me and he said, "There's another friend waiting to meet you over there." I looked over and saw a small car. Inside was a lady, smiling and waving enthusiastically. I walked over to the car through the rain wondering who it could be. As I reached the car she shouted out the cheeriest "Hello, Ralph!" I have ever heard. Then she said something I hadn't heard for years, "Back to the sway." She laughed so merrily that I had to join in. "Back to the sway," was a gag we used at Drury Lane in one of the big musicals I had staged there. At once I realised that this charming girl and I must at some time have worked together. "Fancy meeting you here," I said, still without the faintest idea who my old friend could be. I had to find out, so taking the bull by the horns I asked, "What the dickens are you doing here?" "Doing here? I'm with my husband." I looked at her for a moment, "Your husband? Well, who *are* you?" I shall *never* forget her reply. "I'm Lady Tedder," she said.

How's that for luck? Within half an hour I was drinking tea, smoking and talking to the great Chief himself as if I had known him for years, and within ten minutes I was also sharing a drink with General Eisenhower. Later that night, on our way to visit the Malcolm Club in Tunis, Lady Tedder took me to see Winston Churchill who was recovering from his bout of pneumonia in a house nearby. They had a three circle guard miles from the house and I got through the lot with an out-of-date yellow Air Ministry pass that they wouldn't allow me to enter Adastral House with when I got home even though they knew me. I hope the Air Marshal will forgive me for telling this, but I assure you the next morning I gave the longest and strongest security lecture I have ever given.

Later in the day I had a long conference with Lord Tedder and he told me what he wanted. The ball was right at my foot. I was to get all the help I needed and the boys in Burma would be getting some Gang Shows. I was also to leave for home immediately! "I want three shows ready by the time I reach England," the Chief told me. "For Burma?" I asked. "No," I was told. "Not for Burma, for somewhere else, and I want you with them." I knew then my new job. I had to prepare three new Units to stand by in readiness – for the Second Front.

Nothing seemed to tire Lady Tedder, who took me everywhere during the last few days I remained at Headquarters. Planning, running, opening Malcolm Clubs, one thought was foremost in her mind always – the airman. I often wonder if the boys realised what opposition she had to overcome, but all obstacles seemed to go down before her. More than once I have seen her standing still, watching hundreds of men eating, laughing and writing letters home in a Malcolm Club which never could have existed but for her.

I boarded a plane for HOME! No more blasting heat, no more boiled rice like spotted dog with flies deputising for currants – those things were behind me and I returned to the Air Ministry with instructions from "The Chief". Tedder had sent on signals which told the powers that be I was acting under HIS instructions, and when I reported to my boss, Air Commodore Strang Graham, he greeted me simply saying, "Hello God." The Air Ministry knew exactly what I was supposed to do. I was offered leave, but turned it down; I was far too anxious to get on with the job in hand so that when the Chief arrived back I should be absolutely ready for him. Luckily, at Houghton House we had a small lecture hall in the basement, which my staff had turned into a theatre, and at all hours of the day rehearsals went on without a stop. I had three new Units to get ready for Tedder and nothing was going to stand in my way. I churned out more songs and sketches in those next three weeks than I had ever done in such a short time before. I dragged out my old sleeping-bag from my Boy Scout days and rigged up a bed on the floor of the office. I did not leave Adastral House for days, but the shows were planned long before the Chief landed back in this country. We carried on with the usual routine, giving shows on the home stations, always aware that the big moment was not far away.

Then, suddenly, the Chief was among us and there was much activity everywhere. One afternoon, I had been to see Lady Tedder, and she suggested calling at the Chief's office and having a cup of tea with him. I shall always remember that afternoon. He was sitting at his desk – there wasn't even a postcard on it – and he was smoking his pipe, kidding me and talking of trivialities as though a war was the last thing on his hands. While the whole world was waiting for the greatest moment in living history, here was the Deputy Supreme Commander quietly joking and taking tea as though he had nothing at all on his mind.

When I got back to my own office the fellows there pelted me with questions about when the Second Front was to begin. "There's one thing I can tell you," I said, "It won't be for a bit yet. The Chief seemed as though he had nothing to do."

The Second Front started next morning.

It was now a twenty-four hour day for all of us. We knew that when the order did come it would mean crossing over at a moment's notice. All the Home Units were held in London and there was tremendous excitement about which one would be the first to go. I was kicking my heels in one of the welfare offices when Air Commodore Strang Graham poked his head around the door. "Ralph, you leave for Northolt tonight. The Number One Unit goes over in the morning."

We jumped up and gave a cheer and the Air Commodore shook hands with us all like a schoolboy who had just scored a winning goal. All the other Units helped us on our way but just before we left Kingsway an officer rushed down to tell me that we had to give a show that evening at the Nuffield Club, and leave for the aerodrome immediately afterwards. We had been innoculated that morning and the injections were taking a somewhat drastic effect. During the performance that night we were in agony. Quick changes, and handling those enormous baskets of props, taxed us to the limit and when we finally arrived at Northolt the Unit was exhausted.

On one of the most glorious of summer mornings we left for Normandy. How different it was from what we had expected – so calm and quiet was it after the doodle bugs we had left behind. It almost seemed as though we were going on holiday. It was an impression that very soon passed! There are many who can describe those early days in Normandy, so I'll confine myself to our own activities. We camped in an orchard and gave our first show that afternoon in the open. Planes were taking off and landing all the time and the audience could virtually hear nothing else. However, after watching several air combats and a couple of crashes, we still put on another show in the evening.

Some of my memories of those early days still make me smile and are perhaps worth recording. One hectic night, the guns were banging, the bombs were dropping and there were aerial fights overhead. The sky looked like an old-fashioned Crystal Palace firework display. It was almost impossible to speak as we lay under the lorries in the darkness. Suddenly I saw a sergeant on his knees by the lorry. "Mr. Reader, do you want to see a picture?" he yelled. "What?" I said, – and he repeated his question. Not knowing what on earth he meant, I said, "Sure." The boys and I exchanged glances and one wag said, "What a lovely night to be going to the flicks; let's go in the two-and-fours." Crawling across a field, we reached a small tent. Twenty of us huddled together in a space meant for six, and on a tiny screen about a foot square we saw a movie, *Captain Blood.* With nothing but a piece of canvas above us, with everything that went up bound to come down somewhere, and with a deafening noise like thunder outside, we watched and heard Errol Flynn fight the Armada. Reel two followed reel eight, as reel eight followed reel one, but it didn't matter. It was fun!

At Christmas time, when the Germans broke through the Ardennes, we were doing a show in an incredibly old and ramshackle barn when a despatch-rider burst in. "If you don't hurry, the Jerries will be here before you finish the show!"

Then there was the very mild 'night out' with the Padre – just a couple of drinks and a happy chat. I crawled back under the lorry and just as I was beginning to think I hadn't wakened the sleeping men, Joe Smith whispered to me: "Chief, I'm plastered." "What with, Joe?" "Your breath," he snapped back.

I remember the mad hectic cheering and screaming of the crowds in Brussels. Before long it would be over. This was what we had been waiting for, this the reward for the partings, the fighting and the years of separation. Soon, very soon, it was to end and we would be home. Talking one night to a husky, six-foot-three Scots Guardsman, I asked him what he wanted to see most of all when he got home. His reply was extremely simple: "Me mother."

The end was in sight. Some of the R.A.F. Gang Shows were already appearing in Germany (amongst them the WAAF Gang Shows) and it seemed all over bar the shouting. We were all beginning to think of being demobbed and my number being 10 meant that I would be out very early. One final memory of those days was my going to see my own Number One Unit off to Italy – without me. Jack Healy was in charge and as they boarded the plane at Croydon Aerodrome I said to him, "Son, the next time you see me I shall be in civvies." We shook hands and the plane took off. I went back to the Air Ministry and reported their departure to Air Commodore Strang Graham. He looked at me and said, "Reader, you will now take instructions from ME. You will go on leave for at least two weeks and I don't want to see you here again until that time is up!" I went back to the office, begged Jack Cracknell to ring Northolt to see if there was a plane leaving for Italy. There was and I took it! To the surprise of my Number One Unit, I walked in as they were preparing for their show and said, "Do you need a stooge for the night?" I played in the show and did so for two weeks, and then one unforgettable Sunday evening in a theatre in Naples, with the aisles filled with men sitting on the floor, I played in my last R.A.F. Gang Show. It could not have been a more fitting occasion as it was with my OWN Unit – with Jack, Charlie Viggars, Len Snelling, Joe Smith, the Cox Twins, Arthur Tolcher and all of them. When the curtain fell I knew this was the end of my days with the Service Gang, and Jack Healy, Charlie Viggars and I had a drink together and we hardly spoke a word. This wasn't sentimentality, but it *was* sentiment. We had come through a lot together. We knew that this was the end of an era as far as *I* was concerned and what the future would hold no one could foretell, but with all the years behind us, and with Jack whom I had first met as a fifteen-year old boy in the 10th Hampstead Sea Scouts, it just meant that we were to say a farewell.

I knew I would be returning to England next day and would shortly be getting my bowler hat. The unspoken memories of those war years were flashing through our minds as we sat at that table and drank some Italian wine. We laughed about the time when Cardew Robinson was performing in an outdoor 'theatre' in Normandy and a rocket which was accidentally released from a stationary plane just missed him and went right through the backcloth, exploding a few hundred yards away. Cardew didn't bat an eyelid, except to say to the airmen sitting on the grass, "Whose side are you on? We can't be THAT bad." Typically Cardew. We recalled the night at Hendon when I fell through two tables in full view of the audience of about two thousand and landed flat on my back. We laughed about the time Jack Beet and George Cameron went to a market and kept raising their hands at deals for the cattle and found they had bought ten pigs. (The two of them escaped before the settling time came). We remembered the dozens of times we lost our way to a station when it was an offence for anyone to tell us a direction and we arrived finally when everyone had gone home. We remembered one evening when there was only one person in the audience and I said, "Son, you've come to see the show and we're going to give you the whole thing" and he replied, "Well hurry up sir, I'm the orderly corporal and I want to lock up." We talked about those early days in France when we arrived and a great crowd of soldiers were massed to greet us shouting, "Bring 'em out, bring 'em out" and we discovered that instead of the billing, "RALPH READER AND TEN BLOKES FROM THE GANG SHOW," it was billed as "RALPH READER AND TEN BLONDES." We sat there for hours either talking or silently remembering.

At one time in our wanderings I had told each of our Gang, "If ever I pass by a theatre and see your name in lights, I'll never pretend it was *my* doing, but you'll have to forgive me if I do kid myself that I helped to screw in one of the bulbs." They still accept that.

Incidentally, I wonder how many of my readers know that Gang Shows were produced in the Prisoner of War Camps in Germany? Well, they were, and by a young sergeant, Don Nesbitt, using scripts which we had been allowed to send him. In return, he was able to send me photographs of some of his productions in Stalag VII.

Let me end this section by paying a lasting tribute to everyone of the men and women of the Royal Air Force who worked with me during the war. I hope they can realise how proud I am of them, how proud I was to be one of them. To travel thousands of miles, as they did, with just a sergeant in charge (and he was usually one of the hardest workers both on and off stage), to forget such things as regular hours, to give everything they had for the enjoyment of their serving brothers and sisters, playing sometimes four and five shows a day, was no easy task. I can only repeat the words the Director of R.A.F. Welfare wrote of them: "These men and women did more man-hours, consistently, than any others in our branch of the service. They lived constantly under conditions rarely understood. They travelled for hours through winter nights in open lorries to reach a distant site where a few airmen needed entertainment; throughout the war not one single major charge was issued against any member of the R.A.F. Gang Show. I congratulate them, and I am proud to have had them in my Establishment."

As part of my own personal tribute, I would like to quote from the national and service papers. I think it may prove enlightening. But first, here is a cable which the Air Ministry received from Lord Swinton, the Secretary of State for the Colonies: "My own staff and I saw the R.A.F. Concert Party organised by R. Reader. We all agreed that it was the best entertainment we have had in West Africa. Is it possible to assign them to West Africa for six months? This would be a god-send to all those serving and would incidentally help with the Americans. The great advantage of this R.A.F. party is that, being service personnel, they can go anywhere and stay at any service camp. This is invaluable for "out" stations which are difficult to cater for."

From the Evening Standard, Tuesday February 15th 1944: "They played the Gang Show on board the ships escorting the surrendering Italian fleet. They travelled in lorries between Tripoli and Tunis, and took eight weeks to do the journey, living entirely on corned beef and biscuits, and were once lost in the desert. On the Burma frontier they were caught in three Japanese raids in one day. They have already travelled over 100,000 miles."

From the Air Force News: "In my opinion they can never be repaid for the hard, morale-boosting work they do. A member of the Air Council started an enquiry to find out the average working-day of a Gang Show airman. And it was sixteen hours. Work out for yourself what it must be like over here, where amenities can often be counted on the fingers of a bloke giving the V sign. They're a great bunch – great Scouts."

From the Union Jack: "Their next move was to Palestine, then Syria, then Lebanon, Iraq, Persia and the Persian Gulf, Arabia, India and now Ceylon. Good though it is to see so much of the world, it isn't much fun playing one day in a climate where everyone is muffled up in the heaviest great-coats and then two days later putting on, a show with a temperature of about 90 degrees. One of their big worries is mail. They move so fast it takes some time to catch up with them and they've had none for weeks."

From the Daily Express: "It is the story of concerts taken further into the front line than any entertainers have gone. It is a story, too, of parties struggling through bitter weather to take music and humour to a handful of men in listening posts and remote places."

From The Star: "To date, more than 3,500,000 service men have been entertained in all theatres of war since November '39 by the Royal Air Force's own entertainment, The Gang Show. The players, all airmen, have travelled 339,000 miles in this period, averaging 15,000 miles a year for each show."

It makes me proud to have been able to place on record the work these men and women did during the war and to re-tell some of the tough times they frequently had. The quotes confirm this. Now, though so many years have passed and we are all that much older, I still look upon the members of those wartime Gang Shows as "my boys" and as for those darling girls in the WAAF Gang Shows, well, they will always be my sweethearts. Each year we hold a dinner-dance and if ever you had an opportunity of looking in on that reunion you would understand the spirit that existed amongst them and how positive it still is.

"Bless 'em all!"

12

Civvy Street

The time came to say goodbye to service days, goodbye to the thousands of miles travelling all over the world, farewell to the lecture-giving, to the search every morning in all the daily personal columns of newspapers trying to spot some disguised, innocent-looking few lines that meant a message for an enemy agent. No more waking up to the batman bringing a cup of tea, or brewing one's own in the heat of the desert. It meant leaving behind the comradeship that will never be equalled outside the Services, it meant giving up being a number and becoming a Mr. again. It meant getting into a civvy suit once more and a return to a world that had completely changed. I wonder even today what happened to that spirit which existed amongst us all during those grim five years of war. The years when we all seemed to be a happy breed, a band of brothers. Now it was peace, and for millions a farewell to arms.

I received my 'bowler hat' and then began to wonder how to get back into show business. To my rescue came Tom

Arnold, one of the great theatre managers of his day. He took me to lunch at the R.A.C. Club and suggested that he would like to put out a super production of the R.A.F. Gang Shows featuring myself and the men who had played such a great part in the success of the Units during the war days. We agreed upon terms and then had to wait until some of the essential people were demobbed and available. Meanwhile I had to write the show, but naturally we intended to include some of the major items which had made such a hit with the troops. He spared no expense and eventually a cast of eighty were engaged. I wondered where he intended to open the show and so, one day in his office, I asked him. He immediately said, "Blackpool, the Opera House." Now we were going to open in February when Blackpool is a deserted town. What's more the Opera House is one of the most elaborate theatres in the country and holds over three thousand people. To play there in the month of February seemed to me to be ridiculous. I looked at him and said, "Tom, BLACKPOOL IN FEBRUARY? It would be murder to play in the Opera House for a week when the town is practically empty." He quietly replied, "ONE week? You're going to play there for THREE weeks." I nearly went berserk! Sure I realised that Blackpool had been the home of thousands of airmen during the war, but Blackpool in February and the war only just behind us!!! However, he stuck to his decision and it is now part of theatrical history that for those three weeks we broke the house record. Even at a matinée it was impossible to get seats. Nothing will ever erase the memory of those three weeks from the mind of anyone who appeared in that show – it was, and still remains, one of the most triumphant openings any show has ever had. God bless every landlady in Blackpool! And thousands of airmen will endorse that.

With banners flying, we toured triumphantly on – Glasgow, Newcastle, Manchester, Birmingham and then the West End. After a healthy run at the Stoll Theatre, back the show went again on the road, opening at the Brighton Hippodrome, where they had the police out on Saturday night to control the crowds.

The Brighton Hippodrome! Here, years and years ago, I had come, riding in that old horse and cart with Grandad to sleep in the stable after having watched in this very theatre Marie Lloyd, Little Tich, George Formby, Harry Lauder and Vesta Tilley and all the richest talent of those very wealthy days. Here, as a small boy, my hopes and plans had been laid, the ambition one day to find myself waiting for my call behind those red and gold curtains. Well, it had come off. I was there, not only as a star, but as author, composer and producer of my own show. Every night that week saw me standing outside the theatre watching the customers going in. Along came all my dear old friends from South Heighton, Denton and Newhaven, so pleased, so happy that my luck had held.

There were new ventures ahead, too. Next came *Something to Shout About* and then a super-production for the Royal Air Force which was sent out on tour to assist recruiting. Written by John Pudney, with music composed by myself, *Wings,* with a cast of three hundred, took to the road. The airmen and airwomen in the cast travelled in large coaches from city to city and lived in the R.A.F. Station nearest the town in which the show was playing.

After this show was launched I went back to Blackpool with a Summer Show at the Grand Theatre. The Christmas following I found myself making my first appearance in pantomime – as Buttons in *Cinderella.* Joe Seymour produced it, and my thanks go to him for a lesson in what pantomime should be. He argued me out of a dozen things I wanted to do, and somehow I don't think he was wrong once!

At this time we were approached by Lew (now Sir Lew) and Leslie Grade to form a new Company called "Ralph Reader Ltd." We were to produce shows, some of which I was to appear in, and present various productions including radio programmes. With Bill Sutton at the helm and Jack Cracknell as secretary, we formed the National Light Opera Company, sending out a new edition of *Glamorous Night, Careless Rapture* and several other productions. In the meantime I was again appearing under the Herbert Wilcox banner filming *Derby Day* with Anna Neagle, and even doing a variety act which I am bound to confess was an all-time flop! I headed the bill at the Middlesbrough Empire and it was one of the worst weeks of my life. Even the manager didn't bother to come round to see me. To say I was a flop is an over-rated statement. I was terrible! I had no real variety act and what I tried to do was quite beyond me. It took several years to get that awful week out of my mind. A 'single' in variety is one of the hardest things to do. And I found it out! How I escaped from Middlesbrough without getting lynched I shall never know. Perhaps they didn't think I was worth the expense of the rope. I walked into the office of Ralph Reader Ltd. on the Monday morning realising how limited I was! However, time performs wonders and before long I was beginning to get a return of confidence. Another starring pantomime for the Grades followed this and I was back on my feet again. Bill kept the firm busy with one thing and another and then came an offer to take the first professional concert party to entertain the troops fighting in Malaya. I jumped at this and it was one of the best experiences of my life.

There were four in the party – a pianist, a comedian, a really beautiful girl, Lucille Graham, and myself. We rehearsed for about four days and were ready for the trip. This is the only time in my life I have ever kept a diary, but throughout this tour I wrote daily of our experiences. I took with me the ball used in the Cup Final, thanks to Newcastle United, and Glasgow Rangers and Celtic each loaned me one of their jerseys to show to the Jocks. I compèred the show and, strange as it may seem, the majority of the gags were those I had used during the war and although I was now playing to the sons of those men after the Second World War, every single joke met with the same laughter and applause. The year was 1952 and I think the best way to recall that trip is to quote a few notes from my diary so here goes.

Sunday, May 25th, 1952

I'm wishing myself a happy birthday. Started well by going to early Communion in the little camp church. We were to move on by train but now discover we shall go by road, the C/O laying on necessary transport and guards. Just read at breakfast that the good old Suffolks have done it again and caught the brother of the bandit District Leader. Nice work. Shall be sorry to bid farewell to the Green Howards.

On to Sagarmat. Good journey, but I was seated in the front of an open jeep. What they really might call a sitting target. I kept alert (especially at ambush corners) when I spotted all the guns at the ready, and when I heard the click of Capt. Robbie's revolver as he sat behind me. Good type, Robbie, and what an Arsenal fan. (Has tremendous collection of old programmes and receives regularly the Supporters' Magazine.) Though ten thousand miles are between them, such enthusiasm and devotion to the Gunners squeezes the distance between here and the gates of Highbury to a couple of yards. I hope Tom Whittaker, Joe, the Comptons and the Drakes-to-come can appreciate what they mean to their fans so far away. (Must tell Jimmy Logie and Alex Forbes how many times they have been asked after).

This afternnon I met some grand young Malay boys from a Scout troop here. In their Scout hut on the wall, facing the door, was a picture of myself, taken many years ago. I asked the young P.L. who it was and he said in his broken English that it was the "Scout who wrote songs to get their Scout hut." I felt very humble, for the kid had no idea who I was. The years between have made havoc with the touched up face on the photo, but I'm inviting them all along to the show tonight.

Nearly all Jocks out front tonight and do they know how to enjoy themselves! They cheered as loudly as if the boat were coming to take them home. Biggest crowd we have played to so far; they overflowed outside to the windows, doors and balcony and even back-stage. When I brought out the two Scottish football jerseys they loudly sang "We Will Follow Rangers." They might well have been on the terraces at Hampden.

Must remember to write to young Kanan and Chandra when I return. (These are two Malay Scouts). Looking back on the past twenty-four hours, it's been quite a nice birthday, thank you.

Monday, May 26th

Today we go to Klueng, where we are due for two shows. Managed to deliver the letters for boys from their families – all except one and this for a kid named McIntyre who happens to be spending a weekend with the band at the very spot we are going to. Doubt whether I shall see him as he will be on his way back to his own camp so I've left his letter with the Padre. Have to do this journey in an armoured truck which means we shall be deep down inside the vehicle; unable to see a thing except through the slits in the side and above our heads and even these are half covered with the rifles. Had a sleepless night owing to an open veranda and odd birds perking in, and likewise 'things that creep in the night.' Oh, for England where only an odd owl bothers you. (Lucille badly bumped her head getting into the car at the start. She made no fuss. She is a gal and a half).

We're here. Nowt happened, but it's a nasty road. One very bad bit known to all out here as "Windy Corner." A natural for an ambush and the bandits have scored many a success here. It's a horse-shoe bend with high steep hills on one side, a drop on the other side to several hundred feet and a small narrow wooden bridge to cross which brings speed down to about five miles an hour. Approaching this, the guards were tense, had rifles at the ready and a glint in their eyes which meant business. All went well, however, for a police patrol had got there ahead of us and were camping out. Nevertheless, I was glad when it was behind us.

We are billeted at the R.A.M.C. Officers' Mess, as this is one of the big hospital bases, and we shall be doing shows in the wards this afternoon. The camp has Ghurkas, and a P.O.W. camp full of Chinese Communists (mostly women). As our driver and escort left us to get lunch, I saw a young bandsman and asked him if he knew McIntyre: he said he did. So I've asked for him to be sent over to see me; then I can explain about the letter from his mother which I've left with his Padre.

Lovely quarters here and we don't leave for Singapore until the afternoon of tomorrow, so I'll check up on all my gear, shirts, underwear, etc. Busily doing this when young Jimmy McIntyre showed up. Very nice lad, modest, clean, good-looking type. He was delighted when I told him about the letter. We jawed for about twenty minutes, then I shook hands with him and wished him a good return journey to his camp. I watched him walking off down the road, and he suddenly turned and waved a final cheerio. Dear me, how young some of these boys look.

The ward show's this afternoon; met a couple of lads we had first bumped into on the train going to Kuala Lumpur. They greeted us like old pals. The night show was super and in the front row sat Dorothy from Worcester, a Scouter still, and with her was her hubby who is Scout Commissioner here. Still carrying on the good work, bless 'em. They return to England for a holiday in three weeks' time. Had grim news after the show – apparently our drivers who brought us here hit trouble on the way back. Know no details yet so hope it's not serious. How easily this could have happened to us on the way here. I'm not going to bed for awhile in case news comes through about the boys. Waited until 2.30 a.m. and still no arrivals but C/O says he has word it is not too serious. (I wonder what that really means). He advises me to get to bed and says he'll give me word first thing in the morning.

Tuesday, May 27th

Out bright and early to get news of the drivers. Two are here and not badly hurt. On my way back from their ward a young medical orderly chased after me and said a patient who had been brought in last night wanted to see me. "Who is he? Do you know his name?" I asked. "Yes, sir," said the orderly, "his name's McIntyre." I felt a jar in the pit of my stomach and nearly ran to the ward. There I saw young Jimmy lying on the bed and still not quite clear of the ether from an operation. He looked even younger than yesterday, his eyes closed and his arm bandaged. I sat down by the bed and waited for him to open his eyes. It took him about a quarter of an hour and then without even looking at me he said, "Hello, Mr. Reader." I found out his arm had been smashed rather badly in an accident to the car on the road back. Very quietly I asked him how old he was, and I shall always remember his reply: "Twenty-one, sir." There was a pause and then he added, "Today."

One incident which caused a lot of publicity when we returned is worth remembering. We spent a few days at Kinloss Officers' Mess prior to going into the jungle for a number of weeks. On our return we were again sent to Kinloss but on arriving we were told that, as it was dining in night, we could not dine in the Mess unless we had evening dress. Now let's face it, who would go on a tour such as ours with dinner jackets and the girls with evening dresses. We took deep umbrage about this and, as we refused to eat in our rooms, we decided we would go into Singapore and feed there. It wasn't a pleasant evening because we had done what we considered a fair job and to be treated in such a way wasn't exactly a compliment. However, we tried to forget it.

When we returned home the press were waiting for us and questioned us as to how the boys were, what the trip was like and asked a dozen questions about morale, etc. The party was held in the office of our Company and after a few glasses of champagne one of the girls raised her glass and said, "Here's to Kinloss Mess." Immediately the press said, "What does that mean." We told them. Next day every national newspaper came out with headlines. Here are a few. Daily Mirror: "ROCKET NEEDED Kinloss Mess, Singapore, Ralph Reader with his Company, after a gruelling tour of the jungle camps would like some dinner. Do they get any? No! Why? Because they aren't in evening dress. This is not a skit from a revue. It really happened." Daily Mail: "WAR OFFICE PROBE RALPH READER BAN. Mess incident incredible." Evening News: "JUNGLE SHOW – 'Explain' War Office signal." Daily Graphic: "Jungle Stars banned by Mess." It caused a real commotion and it was certainly not intended by us. However, the War Minister, Mr. Anthony Head, did most kindly send us a note expressing his regret. There were laughs, however, ahead. I went to the Victoria Palace one night shortly after I got back from Malaya and Bud Flanagan suddenly said from the stage, "We're not going on with this show until Ralph goes home and puts on his dinner jacket." It got a roar of applause.

Kuala Lumpur turned out to be a very special spot for us. The three heads in Malaya at that time were Sir Gerald Templar, Colonel Young (Head of the Police) and, second in command, General Sir Rob Lockhart. Sir Rob was the Deputy Chief Scout and I knew him well, so what a joy it was when we arrived there to find a note saying, "We are waiting for you, ring King's House and a car will be sent you at once to bring you here for dinner." And what a splendid time we all had with Sir Rob and his dear wife, Lady Madge. Yes, Malaya and our tour there is another unforgettable memory.

I returned to England to go straight away into rehearsal

for a touring twice-nightly revue and a very successful tour this was. We played the Moss Empire and Stoll Houses up and down the country. The week at the Birmingham Hippodrome, always one of my favourite theatres (probably because we have never lost money there), was an exceptional one, but beyond a doubt, of all the times I have played this house none will ever touch that famous week in 1957 when the World Jamboree was held at Sutton Coldfield and Scouting was celebrating its fiftieth anniversary. It was the first time we had taken the entire London cast on tour and we were sold out three weeks before our opening. Every performance was like a Jamboree in itself. We ended the show singing the *Jamboree Song* which I had written and the volume of the singing from the stage and the entire audience proved at every performance that the Birmingham Hippodrome was solidly built.

I did a lot of travelling not only in England but abroad. I spent four tumultuous weeks in South Africa as a guest of the Scout Association there, with hospitality reaching an all-time high and a memorable visit to Rhodes Tomb, high on the hill with nothing but the sight of mountains as far as the eye could see, was an emotional experience. Sitting on Table Mountain looking down at the lights in Capetown is another thrilling experience and many of the veterans of World War Two will vouch for this. And I wonder how many of them still remember Mrs. Gibson, "The Lady in White," who greeted every troop ship arriving at the port, and on their departure, through that famous megaphone, she sang to them, *Land of hope and glory*. They will remember too her clarion call of "COO-EE" which stretched across the water to the men massed on the in-coming convoys. I met her whilst I was on this visit to South Africa. She had had an accident and had lost the sight of one of her eyes but she was undaunted. She said to me, "Ralph, you remember I always loved the Navy, well now I feel like Nelson." What a spirit this dear lady had.

My annual trip to Chicago to stage their Gang Show was another great event for me. I remember one super crack that came from Bob on one of our visits. We were living in the Morrison Hotel and had a room on the 39th floor. (It was then the highest hotel in America). In the morning when we were dressing I said to him, "One thing about being up so high, there is no noise from the traffic." "You're right," he replied, "But, oh, the noise of those harps."

During this period I was staging the gigantic productions in the open air theatre at Scarborough with the stage on a lake. This sort of thing was right up my street and my imagination could run riot. My first production there was a revival of *Show Boat* and I conceived the idea of having the singer of *Old Man River* slowly coming across the lake and passing the front of the stage before the thousands of people sitting on the banked up seats. One night there was a 'fret' from the sea, which is a sort of fog, and the searchlights couldn't find the boat to illuminate it. He sang and sang and the lights went from up to down, from here to there, but still no sign of the oncoming boat. Finally they caught it just as it arrived in the centre of the lake and the cheers from the audience drowned the song completely. Strange things happen in the name of show business.

Of course by this time the Scout Gang Shows had been revived and were playing all over the world and this meant hours and hours of work for me writing new sketches and songs for each edition. As if this weren't enough, the presentations at the Albert Hall were seeing that I had little spare time. However, I found time to write the script and songs for the launching of the Triumph Herald car. This was a complete departure from the usual type of my activities, but I thrive on this – in fact the only time I ever feel any aches and pains is when I am not absolutely tied up with two or three projects at the same time. I know it's about time I began to slow down, and I do occasionally, but the spurt that follows brings me right back on my toes and the elation I feel does me more good than a dozen doctors. In fact, there are so many things which brighten one's life that I cannot resist passing on one or two that have brightened mine.

Few boys have a quicker wit than the average Cockney. Let me illustrate this by telling you of an incident one night when we were playing at the Golders Green Hippodrome. Lady Baden-Powell, the Chief Guide of the World, came to the show, and when she was talking to the Gang during the Interval she told them that she saw Gang Shows all over the world but when she came to London she always expected the best performances and like a flash she added, "Best Performances, B.-P." Later during the second half of the show I happened to be going through the pass-door as four of the youngsters came off-stage after doing their number. As a joke I caught hold of one of them and said, "I watched you out there tonight. Talk about 'Best Performances, B.-P.' I thought you were terrible." Like lightning the youngster came back with, "Yea? Well, don't forget B.-P. means Blooming Producers too."

On another occasion I was going out front to the Box Office and saw half a dozen of our younger members in the lobby looking at the pictures of the show. Now I always told them they were NEVER to go out front. I was standing at the top of the steps leading into the theatre and to make matters worse they decided not to go round to the stage door but to go through the theatre. This was unheard of. In a line they advanced toward the steps and then they saw me standing at the top glaring at them. Any other kids in the world would have stopped and retreated. Not this lot. They marched towards me and as they got level, the front lad looked at me, flipped his lapel and said, "Press!" And on they went. I said nothing, for a crack like that deserved to win.

It's a rule with our Gang that they never start a rehearsal without coming up to me and shaking my hand. They also do this when rehearsals finish. One night we had a New Zealand

Scouter attending our rehearsal and as the boys came up to me to shake hands I'd say, "Goodnight Jim, Goodnight Charlie, etc." The New Zealander said to me, "How on earth can you remember the names of all these boys?" Standing by us was a twelve-year old from Islington. He looked up at the visiting Scouter and said, "That's a funny thing to say isn't it? Don't YOU remember the names of people you love?" Nobody will ever say anything that could bring a bigger lump to my throat. Can you blame me for saying that it's all been worth it?

We used to run the show two months later than we do now, during the time when fogs blanketed everything in a pea-souper, yet throughout the run of the show not one single member of the Gang missed a performance. At times they slept in the dressing rooms, but at curtain time, even though half the audience were stranded in coaches miles from the theatre, every member of our cast was right there for the opening chorus.

With all my many and varied activities I am hardly ever idle and coping with replies to letters that pour in every day starts the morning with my typewriter sometimes getting almost red hot, and the telephone is ever ready with a ring reminding me of a date to be fixed or bringing me the voice of an unexpected friend who has just arrived in England. I am a happy man and I have every right to be. First and foremost, the major joy of my life is my family – Joan, Bob, William and Stephen. I 'adopted' Bob when he was a young Scout in Islington and he lived with me for many years until he married Joan, the loveliest and dearest girl, who gave us William and Stephen. They live only a quarter of an hour from "Round Corners" and my love for them is something I cannot put into words. Love is a strange word because it stands for so many different things. I never mince words and I never say I "like" somebody if I really LOVE them, whether they be man, boy, girl, or woman. We have to remember there is the love for a father and a son, a brother, a sister, and a real friend, which goes beyond ordinary affection; it is the kind of love that existed between David and Jonathan, so why be self-conscious about using this word if you honestly mean it? If it is ever misconstrued by strange people, well, that's too bad, but it never worries me in the slightest. I am not an intellectual man and I know few intellectuals. I prefer to mix with down-to-earth people who deal in common sense and this, I suppose, is solely because I just happen to be a very ordinary bloke.

Do I believe in God? YES! I'm not a betting man, but this is one certainty you can bet on and you cannot lose. If you have the faith that there IS an after life, that there IS a God who will one day receive you, it MUST make your life a happier one because you know and believe there is to be a tomorrow. Now suppose there isn't, and that when you die you simply go to sleep and that's the end. You won't know you have lost will you? And if you don't know you've lost, you have WON. Won because your days have been made happier because you believed, and that kind of happiness is something even death cannot take away from you. So you see, having faith in God is the one bet you can make – and the ONLY bet – which can never be lost.

There will always be rumours about anyone who is in the public eye, and I am well aware of an accusation that I drink too much. Do I? Let me tell you I can drink when I want to, and I can go for days without touching a drop of alcohol. I enjoy going into a pub with friends and knocking back a few whiskies but there are times when I go into a local and never touch a drop of intoxicating liquor though on-lookers, especially at certain gatherings, keep an eye on me and see me draining a glass. I hate saying to anyone "I'm on the wagon" so a friend of mine tipped me off and told me to order a ginger ale because this LOOKS like whisky, and I have done this on dozens of occasions, merrily looking at some of my knockers and loudly asking the barman, "Same again please." I enjoy seeing the disgusted look on their faces.

I am by no means a teetotaller, but if I drank a quarter of what some people believe I do, my liver ought to be put on exhibition!

Presentations at the Albert Hall still have to be fitted in, and the regulars such as the Burma Reunion and the Festival of Remembrance take up a considerable period of the year in preparation. Through these I frequently get an opportunity of returning to some of the old R.A.F. Stations I knew so well and I'm not ashamed to tell you that I often get a lump in my throat when I return to some of them. Especially Scampton – my favourite Station. Even when riding in a train, as it passes by some isolated, now dis-used airfield, I have a strange feeling inside me and the ghosts of the airmen who once gave it life seem not far away. Grass now grows over the runways and the wind and the rain have blown down the old NAAFI, but as the train rushes by, so do my memories. The R.A.F. was to me a way of life and my pride in this branch of the services will never leave me.

13

Scouting Days

It's about time the record was set straight regarding my Scouting experience because a lot of people have strange ideas as to how I came into the Scout Movement. Some believe I came in 'through the back door,' others have said that I was called in because I could help them (being a professional theatrical producer) with shows to raise money for the Movement, and others have openly said that I was never a genuine active Scouter. So let me give you the low-down straight from the shoulder since it may open the eyes of one or two people and enlighten a few others who are suffering from any misapprehension.

I was living in Denton at the time – a typical little Sussex village which I have mentioned earlier. But what a change you would see if you went there today. A village? It's become a rural town with buses running regularly through it, whereas, in my day, it was not much more than a handful of cottages. Now it looks the size of a small town with streets, roadways and hundreds of houses masking every blade of grass that once grew there. It has one pub, The Flying Fish, and walking out of Denton to the top of a hill you come to South Heighton, another small village which also boasts a pub, The Hampden Arms. Both villages had a Church – Denton a very beautiful one, but South Heighton's was more like a tin hut and situated right next to The Hampden Arms. Consequently, I suppose it wasn't really surprising that The Hampden Arms filled up rather suddenly on Sunday nights immediately after Evensong.

Rose Cottage where *I* lived was directly opposite Denton Church and from our attic (where I slept) one had a fine view of weddings, funerals and grave-stones. There had been a Scout Troop in the village some while back but when I first arrived it didn't exist. Several of my pals and I talked about the possibility of re-starting it, but though we mentioned it to the Vicar we didn't seem to get very far. I had previously had a little experience as a Life-Saving Scout with the Salvation Army in Crewkerne, but it was very limited. Then, one Sunday after Church came great news. The Rev. Kimpston said we would hold a meeting and see just how much enthusiasm there was for re-starting the Troop. The response was excellent and though Mr. Kimpston had not the remotest intention of wearing a pair of shorts himself he said he would give us all the help he could. Next day he went into Newhaven and bought a copy of *Scouting for Boys*. Our first meeting was on a Tuesday night in the old Priory behind the Church. Mr. Kimpston read passages from the book and explained that before we could become Scouts we had to pass the Tenderfoot Test. We successfully achieved this in about ten days and that made us ready for our initiation. None of us had a uniform, but I was lucky enough to be given a uniform of a boy who had been in the old Troop and had since been killed in the war. However, within a week, every boy had purchased a full uniform which made us all ready to take the Promise.

So it was that, at the age of eleven, I was enrolled as a Scout in the 2nd Newhaven, Denton & Heighton Boy Scout Troop. As we couldn't find a Scoutmaster it was decided that for the time being the Rev. Kimpston would take charge until a leader could be found. We were formed into two Patrols and a race began as to which would be the first to get promotion. There was terrific competition and I bought myself a copy of *Scouting for Boys* and read and re-read every yarn time and time again so, luckily, I won the prize of being a 'second'. That white stripe on the pocket of my shirt was the proudest award I ever dreamed of getting, and within a matter of weeks I became a Patrol Leader. Les Prout became the other Patrol Leader and we were away! Within three months I was promoted to Troop Leader and with the help of a chap named Chris Mills, Scoutmaster of the Newhaven Troop, who came over regularly to see how we were getting along, I began to take up the reins and run the Troop myself. Luck smiled upon us and the Rev. Bailey, Vicar of South Heighton, suggested that we could use as our headquarters an old dis-used chapel in Heighton. This was a triumph because the Priory was so small we hadn't room to move, so to the old chapel we went and we prospered. Our numbers had risen to sixteen by this time and we then became bold enough to suggest that we should hold our first Church Parade in Denton Church. 'Dad's Army' had nothing on us and we drilled and drilled, determined to put up a good show. As the day drew nearer, we could almost all turn right at the same time and form two's – we hadn't got to the stage of trying to form fours!

The night before the big day we held a dance to raise funds which we sorely needed and a goodly crowd turned up to support us. The music was supplied by a gramophone so the dances could last only as long as the record and every now and then it ran down because somebody forgot to wind it up. However, it was all taken in good part and everyone voted the dance a success. When we arrived at the last Waltz (which was *Destiny*) we turned down the oil lamps because we thought that was the custom for such an occasion, and I happened to have as a partner a well-known youngish lady from the village who, to be polite, was a trifle on the plump side. I remember she asked me if I could reverse and although I hadn't the slightest idea what she meant I said "Yes." So *she* did and I didn't, but because of her weight she did manage to steer me around so I suppose I must have reversed. At the end of the dance she brazenly gave me a peck on the cheek which apparently did not go entirely un-noticed by one or two of those present. I knew that it was the custom to take home the young lady who happened to have the last waltz with you, but as she lived on the top of Mount Pleasant I ducked out. I wanted to be fit for the morrow.

Sunday morning dawned and I was up bright and early pressing my uniform and begging the clock to hurry up and go round. At half past ten we all met at the Troop Room and it was a good turn out with every boy looking spick and span. The two patrols formed up and with me as Troop Leader heading the parade, we marched out of the old chapel into the street and started on our way down the hill to Denton Church. Most of the boys were in step too. Some of the Heighton folk stood at the doors and windows of the cottages and even applauded us as we marched by. We arrived at the church right on time, with the congregation and a few giggling boys getting their first glimpse of the 2nd Newhaven, Denton & Heighton Boy Scout Troop in all its glory. Suddenly, our eyes were centred on the road just outside the church, for there, written in large white chalked letters in the middle of that road was "WHO KISSED FAT NELL?" I don't know whether I went white or scarlet, but I sure went something. With atomic speed I shouted, "Quick March" and then at the double we ran into the church. To this day, I reckon I deserve the V.C. for getting the Troop away from those accusing words so quickly and for ignoring the few giggles from obviously uneducated people who thought it was funny. The Vicar was no help either as he took for his text, "Be sure your sins will find you out." But God was on my side that morning for during the service it pelted down with rain and by the time we got outside those chalked words were completely washed away. Much later I found out that I was not the only one in the Troop who had kissed 'Fat Nell' and at least four of the Scouts thought the words referred to HIM!

We put on concerts to raise funds and I raked in anyone in the village who had the slightest talent. Mrs. Hibbard who ran the local Post Office and sang (a bit); two young girls who sang duets (off-key); a Mrs. Cobbon who danced, though she was over-age, and one or two wives who couldn't really do anything, but they made up the number. One of these ladies arrived home rather late one night and her husband's supper wasn't ready. He met me one evening and rather gruffly said, "What are you doing with my wife?" I lied and said that she had a lot of talent, but he informed me that whatever talent his wife had belonged to him. She did not appear in any of our other shows! But our little efforts flourished although Hughie Green would have found no 'opportunity knocking' if he had paid us a call. Every joke I remembered from my visits to the Brighton Hippodrome was used and many effects I had seen there I tried to emulate – not often successfully, but I was ambitious. One night in fact proved disastrous. There was a song of the period called *The Rose of No-Man's Land.* It was about the Red Cross nurses and I had a brain-wave (?) We had a sweet girl, Ivy Steel, with a very fine voice, and the idea was that she should dress as a Red Cross nurse and suddenly rise before the audience from behind a screen. To get this effect I used a long plank, which she was to stand on. Each end of the plank had a rope attached and at the introduction of the song, two boys were to pull gently on the ropes and Ivy would slowly appear before an astonished audience and sing. Such a thing as a dress rehearsal was never heard of, but I was clever enough to tell her to take off her shoes so that she would be better able to keep her balance. Ivy obeyed. The moment came and I stood by the side of the stage, which incidentally was made up from table tops on sugar boxes. As the introduction started, I nodded to the boys to pull on the ropes. Now the fact that the plank would sway the moment it left the ground did not occur to me. Neither did I realise that the two boys might not pull exactly at the same time. They didn't! Ivy rose – the plank began to sway – but though fear was lurking in her eyes, she bravely kept on singing. Then! Not only did the plank sway, it started to swing to and fro. This would have been too much, even for an acrobat, and before Ivy got halfway through the first chorus she fell off and landed in the laps of two dear old souls sitting in the front row. The candles which we used for footlights blew out and smoke filled the stage. Not even I could have expected the audience to think this was yet another effect to create the impression of poison gas (though it smelt like it) so for a few moments the show was held up. Ivy came back later and sang the song right through, but this time standing firmly on the stage. No tricks, and even wearing shoes.

I remember another occasion when I was told that a lady in the village, a Mrs. A, could play the piano, so after Mrs. A. I went. She jumped at the idea, but warned me that she only played by ear (an expression I had never heard before). I was elated because all the other pianists I had listened to played with their hands, so this seemed like an outstanding novelty. She was booked for the next concert. However, she DID play with her hands and enjoyed it so much that she never knew when to stop. I swear that night she played for at least three quarters of an hour, and I don't think she would have stopped even then except for the fact that it was near closing time at the Hampden Arms and she didn't want to miss her Guiness.

But they were happy days. I helped Nesta Bailey, the Vicar's daughter, run a Cub Pack we had just started, and this, together with all my other activities, began *slightly* to interfere with my work as office boy at the cement works, and the chief clerk, a Mr. Martin, was hardly enthusiastic about my outside interests. He didn't have much sense of humour and for some reason objected to my desk being constantly cluttered up with various copies of music instead of what he considered should be items connected with my job. He once threatened me with the sack because amongst the pay-sheets for the workers which I had laid on his desk he found a layout for a programme lined up for my next concert. As I said, he had no sense of humour. What's more, he never once bought a ticket to come to any of our concerts.

I ran the Troop for about two and a half years and then Harry Avis took over as our official Scoutmaster. During those years I learned a lot about Scouting and many times I wrote to the Editor of *The Scout* who was then Haydn Dimmock. He always replied with many hints and sorted put many of my problems. Years after I was to meet Haydn Dimmock in person and we became close friends. No man I have ever met in the Movement could talk to boys as he could – he had a magic about him when telling stories that few men are blessed with. And what wonderful books he wrote too.

I remember my first week-end camp. We borrowed a bell tent from an Army unit stationed nearby and camped on some ground near the village of Denton. We thought it right and proper to have a guard outside the tent all night, but this lasted only about a quarter of an hour because the guard said it was too cold. It was cold inside the tent too – in fact we were nearly frozen, but I guess that still happens when the inexperienced camp for the first time. No enemy appeared during the night – at least no human enemy – but we did have a visitor who left an autograph right outside the opening of the tent. It was an inquisitive cow who had come to inspect us, lost interest and walked away, but not before leaving her calling card. I got up in the morning and went outside to blow a bugle to signal for the 'rise and shine' and of course stepped right into – yes, you guessed it!

Eventually I received my warrant as Assistant Scoutmaster, working under Mr. Avis, and as such I remained until I left for Ireland. The night before my departure, a party was given for me, and the County Commissioner for East Sussex, Major-General Watson, came and presented me with a Thanks Badge. Two weeks later a letter he had written that same night and which I still have, was forwarded on to me. It read, "My dear Ralph, How happy I was to be able to present you with your Thanks Badge. You kept your Troop running under considerable difficulties which is the more commendable because of your youth. I venture to say that as long as you remain in Scouting, and I believe you will, you will always be able to say that no member of our Movement will receive a Thanks Badge at such an early age as you have done." At the time I was not quite eighteen. Since then I have been awarded the Medal of Merit, become a Rover Leader and eventually Commissioner for London Rovers, and held a warrant as Scoutmaster of the 10th Holborn Troop which I formed. Later I became an Assistant County Commissioner for London and then ran a Sea Scout Group, the 20th Holborn. Every week-end I was out on the Thames in charge of a crew, rowing for an hour before breakfast. In 1938, I received on behalf of the Chief Scout of the World, the highest award in Scouting, the Silver Wolf. This was presented to me by Lord Somers at the Royal Albert Hall. In 1957, came my most important appointment – Lord Rowallan made me a Chief Scout's Commissioner!

It still remains a puzzle to me how I managed to fit in all my Scouting programmes with the various shows I was producing in the West End, coupled with contracts in America which meant my going there at least twice a year. The annual Rover week-ends at Hatfield; the summer camps with my own Troop, the 10th Holborn; travelling all over the country running Camp Fires; accepting guest appearances at unlimited dinners and giving talks at Scouts Own on Sunday mornings up and down every county and covering Ireland, Scotland and Wales. And in those early years, as all my friends will confirm, I did not accept one penny for train fares or any other form of expenses. It was in show business I earned my money and it was on Scouting I spent it. Gladly! (To-day it is different and I do get help, for which I am truly grateful.) "To give and not to count the cost" was the rule in those days and many bank managers to-day would be happier if some of their clients had not been such devoted Scouters. But money can never compete with happiness. Those who have both can count themselves lucky, but I find it easier to count my blessings than count my pennies.

During these great Scouting years of mine I got to know our Founder, Baden-Powell, very well and as long as there is life he will be remembered as the man who founded the greatest Youth Movement the world has ever known. I have spent week-ends at Pax, Bentley, with him and his dear wife, Olave Lady Baden-Powell, Chief Guide of the World, and to me she will always be my favourite pin-up girl. Even B.-P. himself could not surpass her when it came to holding a crowd. Who will ever forget the night when she spoke at the ending of the Sutton Coldfield Jamboree in 1957, celebrating 50 years of Scouting? Thousands upon thousands of boys of all ages stood in the arena listening to her final speech to close that wonderful occasion. Boys from all over the world, many of them not understanding a word of English, knew exactly what she was telling them. Not a sound was heard except the voice of this fantastic lady, and everyone knew she was speaking not to the thousands but to each and every single one of them. At the end of the talk, she told them to go back to the world they came from and take with them the Spirit of Scouting. Then, at her command, they about turned and marched off into the darkness from that mighty arena to their own camp sites, all singing the Jamboree song. The singing faded into the distance until the arena was completely empty, but on the platform remained Lady B.-P. with her hand still raised in the Scout salute.

I remember one evening when I was staying at Pax, the Chief said to me just before he retired, "Ralph, I shall meet thousands of boys more than you, but you will perhaps KNOW more boys than I shall know." Lady B.-P. reminded me of this the last time I had lunch with her at Hampton Court. Letters they have both sent me from time to time remain some of my most precious possessions.

I have written through the years various Scouting plays which have been performed over and over again – such plays as *Great Oaks, The Road to Where?, The Wingate Patrol* and many others and often certain people have said cynically, "Where does Reader get this inside knowledge of Scouting that he puts in his plays?" NOBODY gave it to me, I learned it at first hand from my own Scouting experience. I wish they would remember that I was in Scouting when Scouting was a boy, and the title I value more than any other is, "Skip."

I hope I have now proved that I served my apprenticeship in Scouting and that I am no amateur. The years have rightly brought many changes to the Movement, especially in the past few years. Some I think are great and others I am not so sure about, but no word of criticism will come from me because I firmly believe that if a family has disagreements, then they must be discussed behind the closed doors of their own home and not in front of the neighbours. I might be just as wrong as they may not be right!!

My mind boggles with the memories of the hundreds of Camp Fires, the camps in many parts of the world, and the talks given at all kinds of meetings. I remember my very first address given at the request of B.-P. at a Gilwell Reunion. It was all Scouting and Scouting was then a game. I remember the night hikes with my Troop when a young Cockney lad, Bill Larner, would hold on to my belt whilst I was telling them made-up stories about ghosts as we walked along the lanes and fields near midnight, scared to death that one of the ghosts would suddenly come and get him. When we returned to camp one night I asked him, "Can I have my belt back now, Bill?" He said, "Yes Skip, but next time take us to the Arsenal."

I recall a scene in *Boy Scout* at the Albert Hall when we had about fifteen hundred boys in the arena. I was standing high up on one of the gallery rails looking down and I saw a small boy raise his hand. I shouted down, "What's up, son." He called back, "Skip, I've lost one of my garter tabs." I yelled back at him, "Son, with fifteen hundred boys jammed in that arena, who do you think is going to notice you've lost a garter tab?" Back came the classic remark, "My mum." Stories? I opened an exhibition once in Glasgow and afterwards went around to look at the various stalls and exhibits. I came across a table filled with books and right in front was a book of songs I had written with a large photograph of myself on the cover taken about 20 years earlier. Behind the counter was a dour young fourteen-year-old Scottish Scout. I saw him look at me, then at the picture, then back at me and then, frowning, back at the photgraph. I thought to myself, I'll stick this one out, so I leaned forward over the counter. He did the same and put his nose within an inch of mine. Then he quietly whispered to me, "Ralph, you must have led a terrible life."

There is another amusing remark I shall always remember. I was helping with the British contingent who were attending the American Jamboree in 1937 in Washington. On the final Sunday night a service was held in the open park and there must have been somewhere in the region of sixty thousand people there. It was done in typical American style and, to suit all branches of religion, *seven* sermons were preached. In order that there should be some lighter side to the service, one of the popular singers of the day, a Mr. Lanny Ross, was engaged to sing a few songs now and then to act as a "link" between the various hymns and sermons. He went down well! In fact after about four hours when Dr. West, who was running the Jamboree, said something about, "The wonderful, inspiring, enlightening service is gradually coming to its end" the cheers from the boys were deafening. Eventually, the end did come, with the singing of *Abide with me* and then a closing prayer. Instead of the thousands of boys leaving the arena they all stood up and shouted in unison, "WE WANT LANNY ROSS, WE WANT LANNY ROSS." Later that evening, a young Canadian Scouter asked if I had been to the service. (I had for about an hour, then went into Washington and had a feed, a walk around and returned to the camp where the service was still progressing stronger than ever, although there was a noticeable fidget amongst some of the Scouts sitting on the grass who had already stuck it out for over three hours). Anyway, I told the Canadian that I *HAD* been to some of it and then I asked him if he had been and, if so, what did he think about it. His slick reply was, "Ralph, it was a competition between God and Lanny Ross and Lanny Ross won."

I had a great experience a few years ago when I was invited to visit South Africa by the Boy Scouts Association there. What a splendid four weeks it turned out to be! The many letters I received after I returned home made me feel that all the hard work by so many people, that had contributed to the success of the visit, had been well worthwhile.

Perhaps of all the letters I have had during my lifetime I value most one which was not even written to me. It was sent to Mr. Hubert Martin, one of the all-time great British Scouters. He was our International Commissioner, County Commissioner for Middlesex, Member of the Scout Council, and regarded throughout the Scouting world with a respect second to none. He enclosed the letter with a brief note attached on which he had written, "I want you to keep this letter, Ralph, and read it as often as you can because I consider it an important thing for you to do." The writer who had sent the letter to Mr. Martin had attended a performance of *Boy Scout* at the Albert Hall and these are some of the words he wrote. "I have seldom felt so inspired. I think Hitler and Mussolini would have been shaken too. But what a power for good or evil Ralph Reader has – what a responsibility to be born with. How merciful that he is a Scout." Dear Hubert Martin, I can tell you that I have never taken an important step in my life nor made any vital decision without either remembering or reading again those words.

I ask you to forgive me if it seems presumptious to have written so much about my Scouting life, but my most severe critics are people who have never met me and I just wanted to open their eyes.

Oh, Happy Scouting Days!

14

Summing Up

In this changing world it's impossible not to look back now and then and compare the years behind us with the years that are with us now. Times are bound to change but I often wonder if there was the need to have quite so many changes as we've seen in the past five to ten years?

Standards? To me they seem to have dropped quite a lot. I don't consider myself an old fogey who resists progress, but I do insist that whatever progress we make, a standard must be kept up. Standards of behaviour are essential and things that are happening in what we now call the permissive society fall far below these standards. Everybody is screaming for freedom, but freedom isn't free, it has to be worked for, and too many people are not realising their responsibilities. We place the blame on the government, on parents, in fact on most everything except ourselves. The lack of discipline is obvious, and this is not only in the youngsters. Now let me impress upon you before I say what is in my mind that I appreciate only too well the great contribution made to our welfare by psychiatrists, but there are far too many *amateur* psychiatrists who ought to go and *see* a psychiatrist. I believe discipline went out when psychiatry came in. Perhaps one should call this breed the do-gooders. Imagine three or four young fellows strolling along the street and seeing a complete stranger coming towards them. They decide on a 'mugging' and within seconds this unknown finds a flick-knife stuck into his middle. These ruffians know full well that when they are brought up in Court somebody is going to stand up and defend them by saying that the victim had no right to go walking in the street with such a weak stomach! I believe in meeting toughness with toughness. Never the birch, never capital punishment, but a tough, hard sentence which will make others think and be a genuine punishment for the offence. Leniency breeds contempt and if we are ever going to stop the violence and terror surrounding us today – and in every walk of life – hard punishment must be the rule. You cannot have liberty without responsibility.

Religion is becoming a back number and it will never be brought back to the drifters from our Churches by gimmicks. For the life of me I cannot understand why they decided to have yet another modernised translation of the Bible. Nobody has ever suggested we should re-write Shakespeare. Do we assume he is more important? Call me what you like, but I think the highest standard of living is still set forth in the Ten Commandments, and the greatest reading of all time is the Sermon on the Mount. I'm not pushing the clock back two thousand years, for those two things I have mentioned are as modern as tomorrow. The ten original Scout Laws, too, take some beating, and I am far from sure that some of the changes in them have not turned out to be to the detriment of Scouting.

I've learned what wealth there is in memories and few men can have more than I. I value the letters and the notes written to me over the years, including one from Archie Boyle referring to my war service, which he sent when peace in Europe was declared: "When I heard the news this morning I thought of you. Probably only you and I will ever know and appreciate (proudly and perhaps conceitedly) how the idea began, how it developed and what it really has meant . . . .because of you and perhaps a little because of me." I am proud too of having letters of appreciation in respect of the Gang Show from all five of our Chief Scouts. I keep them in a small case and now and then read them through. From B.-P. our Founder and Chief Scout of the World; Lord Somers; Lord Rowallan; Lord Maclean (now the Lord Chamberlain), and recently a splendid letter from our present Chief, Sir William Gladstone.

The photographs I have in every corner of my home prevent me from ever being lonely. Each one represents someone who has made a contribution to my life. Boys, now grown to manhood with a family of their own, still remember me, they phone me and they often come to visit me. You can never tell what you have done for a boy until you realise what he has done for you.

I remember so often the first production of *Boy Scout* at the Albert Hall, our three appearances at the Palladium in the Royal Command Performance, the first time the R.A.F. Gang Show played in Africa to the Americans and how scared we were as to whether our type of show would suit them. It was one of the most thrilling experiences we have ever had. When Americans like you they have no inhibitions about showing it and the tumultuous applause they gave us when we reached the Finale still rings in my ears. Next day the American issue of Bonjour wrote: "R.A.F. GANG SHOW IS TOPS." They ended their review with these words: ". . . .Yes, men of the R.A.F. and cast of the 'Gang Show,' the men of the Armed Forces of the United States owe you a debt of gratitude for the most splendid entertainment yet seen in this area. It is the best EVER seen by this writer. Gestures, such as yours, in presenting your show for us, bring the men of the Allied Forces into closer relationship, one with the other, and make us more determined to fight together until our every goal is reached. Many Bloomin' thanks, Blokes."

I think back on the happy times I had in Chicago, for there I met one of the great Scouters of all time, Alden Barber. He is now the Chief Scout Executive of the American Boy Scouts.

I remember a young boy who became a fighter pilot and carried his Gang Show scarf with him on every sortie. I met him in Normandy and arranged to see him the following night. Instead a Padre came to me with a red scarf. He hadn't taken it with him – he was shot down that afternoon.

There were other sad happenings too that stir my memory now and then. Whenever the name of Neville Heath is mentioned my mind goes back at once to his victim – a charming girl named Margery Gardner. Margery was a film extra who took part in one of my Albert Hall Pageants. I remember during a rehearsal I invited her to join me for tea. We talked for quite a while and she seemed to me to be a very quiet and kind type of girl. Every night when rehearsals ended she would come over to say goodnight, and if I wasn't too busy we'd chat over a cigarette. She said to me one evening, "I don't think I've ever been so happy as I've been in this Pageant. Everyone has been so kind, it's just like a big family." I said to her, "What am I, the grandfather?" She laughed and then very quietly said, "No, you're just Ralph." On the last night of the show she waited by the stage-door and as I came out with Sir Malcolm Sargent she pushed a packet of Players into my hand and said, "Thanks, it's been fun." Before I could thank her she walked quickly away. I didn't see her again.

There was the occasion when my Scouts and I were camping one week-end in the grounds of a Remand Home where I frequently go to visit the Head and chat with the boys. At these camps, several of the privileged youngsters are allowed to camp out with us. A boy, *not* on the privileged list, delivered the milk each morning for our early tea and I often talked to him as we got the dixie boiled. Just as we were leaving at the end of the camp, I found a small packet addressed to "Mr. Ralph." Inside was a packet of ten Woodbines. With the help of the Assistant Head we found it had been left in the office by the milk-boy; he had climbed in through the window, leaving the cigarettes on the desk. I sent for him and was allowed to see him alone in the office. I asked him why he hadn't put his name on the present and he said, "Because I didn't think you'd take them if you knew they were from me." I went into his story and whatever he had done seemed to me excusable in the light of the home-life he had been brought up in. I kept in touch with that youngster. He is now a sergeant in the Army and holds the Military Medal.

But we cannot build the future on the past – it is what we do TODAY that matters. We are not getting our sights right. Some people will spend hours going to Kew Gardens to worship the flowers there and yet can't find enough time to water the primroses in their back garden. I am entirely with the young girls and boys today who dress in weird outfits and the boys who wear long hair. If they want to be 'with it' then why not let them. (Let's remember that way back in history even kings wore long hair. King Charles for instance. Mind you, they had a cure for it in his day, they cut his head off.) The tide will turn and it would never surprise me if suddenly a Yul Brynner cult starts and all our youngsters will be sporting bald heads. Fashions will change and let's be thankful that we don't see girls wearing bustles. Life would be that much duller without the sight of pretty legs.

I enjoy 'mod' music, though some of the songs high in the charts are beyond me, but there is no doubt that a lot of music composed by the modern generation is real composition as exciting as anything written by the classical composers and may well live as long. Say what you like about the Beatles and the Stones but they have made a contribution far beyond what a lot of us will admit. I think the hero-worshipping of certain groups and pop singers goes too far – too many of them have voices like a slate pencil – but there are others who are a delight not only to hear but to see. Let's not forget the dozens of records we bought in our young days of the Old Groaner, Bing Crosby, and even further back the thrill it gave to millions when they heard the recording of Ernest Lough singing *O for the Wings of a Dove*. WE had our moments too, so don't let us deny the right of the new generation to have their favourites. We need personalities like Jimmy Saville, whatever colour his hair may be, and if the so-called teeny-boppers swoon at the sight of Donny Osmond I remember doing almost the same thing when I first saw Mary Pickford.

Once we had the booming voice of General Booth denouncing the demon drink, today voices are not raised loud enough to force something to be done about the mis-use of drugs. One great step forward would be to make more of our houses, HOMES.

Most kids today like noise, the only thing they are afraid of is silence. Teenagers today like to be heard and that is their right, but they should recognise that the older generation have a right to be heard too. I'm fully aware that because of some of the things I have written there may be people who feel like throwing poisoned arrows at me, but first of all let them make sure they aren't using boomerangs!

So there it is, one life, mine. ONE life? Maybe, but it has been shared with countless thousands. All those who have appeared in the many Pageants at the Albert Hall, the untold thousands in the uniforms of the Royal Navy, the Army and the Royal Air Force I met during the war, and then those thousands of boys the world over wearing another uniform who have filled my life with the devotion of their friendship through all my wonderful years. Regrets? Yes, a few I suppose, but I'd have to give it a lot of thought before I could remember them. I count myself as one of the luckiest men in the world. Would I have had it any different? Let me sum it all up with the final words of a song I always sing at the last night of our Gang Show:

"I wouldn't change for a man with a million
For I've had a million blessings more."

247